AF564486

Organisation Management

DPH Management Series

Organisation Management

J M DEWAN • K N SUDARSHAN

DISCOVERY PUBLISHING HOUSE
NEW DELHI-110002

Discovery Publishing House
4831/24, Ansari Road, Darya Ganj
New Delhi - 110 002 (INDIA)

Organisation Management

Reprinted-2011

ISBN-81-7141-340-4

PRINTED IN INDIA

Printed at Mehra Offset Press, Delhi

Preface

The management world is in transition. The causes of this transition are many, but the major one is the vast changes in knowledge and in the information that flows in and out of organizations. This changing information disrupts traditions, established processes, well-known procedures, and routine ways of doing things. New principles, concepts, techniques, ideas, expressions, processes, and procedures are emerging, moving us to a new plateau of professional practice. Trying to capture this changing knowledge and information is like trying to capture the atmosphere. How can you do it when the atmosphere is continually shifting and when you need the atmosphere to do the capturing? The best we can do is find a peak from which we can at least get a perspective on management as a whole, decide on the work and responsibilities of management, and gather in whatever practical management information we can. A team of experts in this series represent some of the best contemporary thinking and information available. They represent many major successful corporations, active consulting agencies, and well-known educational institutions, and all are experts on what is happening with the flow of knowledge and information in the management world. This is a lofty pinnacle from which to survey the management world.

Managers and supervisors clamor for current information and guidelines to help solve formidable problems in their work world—problems that range from "how to do it" to "how to resolve conflict when doing it." Many problems are generated from miscommunication and incompetence. As the management practice proceeds from the complex to the supercomplex, problem solving becomes a large-scale challenge requiring new knowledge and skills. Managers and supervisors cannot wait for research breakthroughs with real-world answers to solve these dilemmas. They must tackle them here and now with the useful information and proven practices immediately available. Whether making a decision, solving a problem setting up a procedure, designing a process, or resolving a behaviour conflict, a manager must rely heavily on information. To a great extent, management practitioners are information workers; that is, they generate, distribute, store, retrieve, and consume information. Competence in finding and using the right information at the needed time determines to a considerable extent competence in the management function, activity, or responsibility. The *DRH Management Series* attempts to fill this need for usable information in spite of the changing nature of its subject.

The *DPH Management Series* not a book to be read and later discarded. It is a reference book, a tool to be used by managerial personnel in the day-to-day work of an organization. Like a tool, it should never be more than a reach away when a new situation emerges that demands its use. This series aim to achieve a first-and practical and proven knowledge and information as a self-development opportunity for those who are moving into or upward in management. A complete spectrum of management subjects is immediately available for orientation, study, analysis, assimilation, and problem solving. Within one set of covers is the view of management as a totality. The management field is loaded with ideas that the organization of this handbook series unique logic. It follows both levels and areas of responsibilities of an organization.

The work of this handbook series is the collaborative effort of many outstanding people in the management field. The motivation for this work varied from individual to individual, but the central motivation that united us all was the excitement of capturing the management state-of-the-art and sharing it with colleagues in the dynamic profession of management.

This series should be of great help to managerial practitioners at any organizational level who are responsible for a function, department, or set of responsibilities. The handbook series will also give these practitioners insights into management roles and approaches in other areas as well. The subject matter encompasses top, middle, and lower management. Special emphasis was placed on managing people, time, space, budgets, and resources to give the handbook extra utility for middle and lower management. Students of management in university or educational institutions will find the series an invaluable resource for adding "real world" practices to their academic and theoretical foundations. MBA students will gain an invaluable overview of the total organization to complement their MBA degree. Administrators and public managers can become acquainted with practices employed by managers and supervisors in private organizations. These practices are not always directly applicable in public sector bodies, but with thought and modifications, these private practices can adapt to public organizations. Public and university librarians will find the handbook an indispensable reference for the multitude of questions on many topics from the general public, special groups, associations, and students.

Editors

Contents

1 What is an Organisation ?

Organisations are often defined as collections of individuals seeking common goals. We then attempt to ascertain the common goal being sought and look at the elements in the environments in the environment needed for goal attainment. This is useful in underdeveloped nations characterized by small, comparatively simple units. But in complex societies where organisations are huge and highly specialized, this approach breaks down. For instance, can you state the goal for General Motors that is shared by all of its members?

A key feature of organisations is their ability to act as a collectivity. Recognizing this we define an organisation as any collection of individuals that can enter into a legally binding contract. The legal capacity to make contracts is used because it requires: (1) that the entity be recognized by others; and (2) that it can act as a collectivity.

This definition helps resolve a sticky problem in organisation theory. Complex systems are typically broken down into major components. These components are treated as if they were organisations. If the unit can act as a collectivity we think this treatment is appropriate. State universities typically have this legal capacity even though they are only part of the state government. Likewise, wholly owned subsidiaries have contractual capacity and are frequently treated as organisations.

Organisations can be classified as complex or simple. We may call an organisation complex when it contains more than one unit with contractual capacity. If none of its components possesses this legal capacity, separate from the whole, the organisation may be called simple. Thus, ITT, Xerox, and Exxon are complex organisations. So are the departments of Health Education and Welfare, Housing and Urban Development, Defense, and Interior. Most local churches are simple organisations as are local government agencies.

If a unit is part of an organisation but does not possess legal contractual capacity it may be called a subsystem, department, or group. For instance, a state university has an auditing department that reports directly to a board of trustees.It's not an organisation but a subsystem of the university. Units that are recognized externally as collections of individuals but which lack legal contractual capacity are referred to as aggregations or special interest groups. Some units are formed by one or more individuals and/ or organisations to accomplish a specific, limited, and short-range objective. Thompson calls these complex configurations. They may have some ability to act as a collectivity. But that ability is frequently limited by sponsoring organisations. Examples of complex configurations include joint ventures or cooperative projects among government agencies. In the construction industry such cooperative ventures are the rule, not the exception. They are also common in oil exploration and basic research.

The organisation and its specific environment

Our definition of an organisation would apparently lead to straightforward rule for separating it from its environment. What is inside an organisation is that legally controlled by the system. However, this simple rule quickly leads to problems. Individuals, for instance, are typically members of many organisations. Let's use our legalistic approach after developing the notion of domain. Then we will modify the simple rule to include the complexity of defining the boundaries of an organisation.

The domain of an organisation

The domain of an organisation is the set of claims it makes over societal resources. To explain the notion it is necessary to briefly outline the elements organisations often attempt to control and how they may support their claims. What can an organisation attempt to lay claim upon? The literature concerning organisational characteristics suggests the following: goals, outputs, property, technology, structure and members. Earlier we introduced the notion of means-ends chains. We argued it was possible for an organisation to take the overall social function of the system and devise a mission statement. From the mission statement more specific goals could be developed and from this point a strategy for goal attainment could be derived. The strategy would indicate the mix of property, technology, structure, and members needed to create and/or distribute specific outputs. We suggested that organisations that limit their social contribution and develop clear-cut means-ends chain have a better chance for survival. Our arguments centered on the benefits from economies of scale and the synergy received from using related resources. Now we are going to expand the arguments without relying upon the mission of the system as the driving force behind the strategy of an organisation.

It is comparatively easy for an organisation to claim control over goals, outputs, properly, technology, structure, and individuals. Although it's quite another matter for an organisation to actually control any control any of the elements. For an organisation to use any one of the elements, it must exercise some degree of control over it. For instance, members must be willing to work toward organisation effectiveness and goals, follow the structure, and produce the desired outcomes. To gain some degree of control an organisation must back up its claims. It can secure some control with an exchange of resources. For instance, a business hires labor. Organisations can also back up their claims with ideology or a combination of ideology and resources. Let's say the Cub Scouts of America ask parents to volunteer to help all boys in a pack to learn important skills and values. Ideology is preferred since it costs less than tangible resources. The closer the claim to the mission of the organisation, the larger the ideological component can become. In no case does the organisation obtain complete control. The more control desired, the larger the cost in terms of resources and ideology.

The concept of domain highlights several important notions about organisations. One, organisations often claim more territory than they are willing to back up with resources and ideology. Two, outsiders may give an organisation more "control" than it wants." For instance, many critics of business argue that pollution control, decaying cities, and the development of equality in employment should be organisational goals. Parents may assume that public schools know t educate children. Thus, the domain is at the same time larger and smaller than desired by the organisation. Three, a claim over a particular element only continues as long as it is backed up with resources and/or ideology. Once a claim is made it must be continually supported, since the value of resource exchanges and ideology decay over time. We should note this also holds for goals. For instance, government may claim jurisdiction over police protection. If ineffective, however, vigilante groups may contest this aspect of the government's domain and claim it as part of their domain. Claims over goals establish expectations on the part of subgroups in society. Even organisations given exclusive jurisdiction over goals must provide some valuable output or face competition. Let's take a closer look at competing claims over key organisational elements.

The Boundary of an Organisation. The outer limit of an organisation's domain is often called its boundary. At the boundary, control over internal elements is often contested. It may be difficult to clearly separate one organisation from another or delineate control from mere influence. Starbuck has recognized this by likening the organisation to a cloud. At times one cloud is clearly visible and distinct, even though its shape continually changes as it moves across the sky. Two clouds may partially overlap and even merge. It may be impossible to say a particular water droplet belongs to one cloud or another. With organisations, the problem is even more difficult. You are dealing with a large number of elements and potentially different areas of control.

Let's return to our decision rule and modify it. Originally, we stated that an element is inside an organisation if it's legally controlled by the system. Let's refine that. An element is inside the system to the extent that it is legally controlled by an organisation and to the extent that these claims are accepted by other individuals and institutions in society. Obviously, this is not a precise definition. But it appears to be a workable approach to drawing boundaries.

Defining the specific environment of an organisation

Let's restate the basic theme. To maintain control

over internal elements an organisation must continually replenish its resources and maintain its ideological legitimacy. The specific environment is the set of external organisations, individuals, and institutions that a given organisation interacts with. An organisation does not exert legal control over these entities, though it may enter into legal contracts with them. These external units are contracted to enhance the probability of growth and survival as a result of an organisation's domain choice.

The primary units in the specific environment of an organisation are its input suppliers and output distributors. Without their support it would be unable to function. Organisations need assured sources of labor, money, raw materials, and equipment. They need distributors and customers to keep the system operating. This is done either directly via exchange of resources for products and services or indirectly via exchange with a supplier for service to a particular client group.

The organisation also interfaces with competitors. We most frequently think of competitors as those offering similar products and services. But organisations face competitors in other areas as well. There is competition for inputs and outputs.

Less well recognized are a number of institutions that develop as a result of organisations attempting to claim jurisdiction over a particular element. As organisations lay claim to labor, unions and professional organisations are likely to develop to offset organisational control. Slowly, large complex organisations are beginning to realize that their claims for control help span special interest groups. Who protects a "free good", such as air, if organisations claim they can use it as they see fit? First came the development of special interest groups.Now the U.S. government claims jurisdiction and limits the manner in which air can be used. Who ensures individual consumers will receive fair treatment from huge corporations? Currently, there are several interest groups pressuring the government to establish a new agency to work toward this end.

Thus, the government is a potential member of every organisation's specific environment. As the allocator of power it can establish organisations or eliminate them. However, the U.S. government is not a single organisation. It is a complex configuration composed of a number of organisations. They compete with one another in a manner not dissimilar to businesses. However, the focal point of the competition often rests with goals and values, not products and services.

So far we have identified suppliers, distributors, customers, special interest groups, and the government as members of an organisation's specific environment. Each of these has been related to the attempts of an organisation to gain control over its internal elements. There is another group of institutions in the specific environment that most organisations tend to dismiss. These are organisations operating in areas not directly related to their mission or domain. Many of these organisations have a different social function. They become a part of an organisation's specific environment because each is part of the larger society. For example, business organisations support charities and universities. Universities, in turn, lend technical assistance to business and government agencies. Churches may provide public schools with meeting rooms. The list is almost endless.

Immediate payoff in not automatically expected in many contacts between institution with different social functions. Many of these contacts appear to be made to improve the image and legitimize the organisation. A few, however, may have direct payoff. For instance, large corporations are most likely to give money to a prestigious private university where their top executives hope their children might attend and from which they hope to obtain new employees. Such "gifts" are often publicized as evidence of the corporation's social responsibility. Universities often lend assistance to local governments as part of their "service obligation to the community." The fact that such help enhances the probability of greater state funding by local legislators is rarely mentioned.

For a large corporation the number of external individuals, organisations, and institutions composing its specific environment can run into the thousands. Even simple organisations may have a specific environment with hundreds of units. But only a comparatively few units in the specific environment receive very much attention by top management. Those external units that do receive attention from the organisation appear to have an impact on its internal operations and decision-making structure.

The Enacted Portion of the Specific Environment. Weick argues that organisations only respond to those external forces that are enacted. That is, the system responds to those elements that demand its attention. Not all the institutions just described demand attention. And most managers in complex organisations face only a few portions of the specific environment. The literature on organisational environments splits on this key issue. Is the entire set of units comprising the specific environment important, or just those recognized by the system? While there is no clear-cut answer the following seems reasonable.

Some portions of the specific environment are more important than others. Different portions of the specific environment are relevant to different managers. The system cannot respond to environmental pressures that remain undetected. Thus, we expect alterations in the domain of the organisation to be partially explained by managerial perceptions. That is, the organisation responds directly to the enacted part of the specific environment.

Conditions in the specific environment of the system probably have a direct impact on organisational outcomes whether they are perceived by managers or not. For instance, even if an organisation does not see consumer resistance to a product, sales may suffer. Thus, the objective aspects of the specific environment are important when predicting organisational success.

Managerial perceptions of the specific environment do not automatically correspond to more objective descriptions. However, it appears more likely that managerial perceptions and objective descriptions of the major units in the specific environment will become increasingly similar as you higher into the managerial ranks.

The definition of an organisation as a legal entity should be carefully noted. Assume you are attempting to describe the specific environment of a simple organisation, Sasquash Division, of a complex organisation, Diversified Creatures. The perceptions of the important units in the specific environment of the head of sasquash Division are likely to be very similar to objective measures for the division. It's unlikely, however, that the division head of Sasquash knows very much about the specific environment of Diversified Creatures.

There may be a large overlap between the "enacted" environment and the actual environment when top-level decision makers are asked to describe important outside forces. Lower-echelon managers, however, probably have more difficulty in accurately assessing external pressures. They have a difficult time seeing the "big picture." But regardless of whose perceptions are used, we need to answer a critical question: Which are the most important units in the specific environment?

Important Units in the Specific Environment. We have asserted that supplier, distributors, competitors, and government agencies are particularly important. They have a direct bearing on the short-run survival of the organisation. Let's go a little farther.

If you accept the notion that exchange is the basis for interaction among organisations, it is quite obvious that most individuals or special interest groups have comparatively little to offer organisations. In the case of individuals an organisation can readily substitute one person for another. Special interest groups have difficulty mounting the sustained effort needed to alter existing conditions. Their claims over internal elements may be heavily weighted toward ideology. At the first sign of progress, members of special interests are likely to switch their affiliation to other groups. Unlike organisations, success may spell the death of a special interest group. For example, in the mid 1970s, a loose coalition of housewives boycotted meat to protest dramatically rising costs of beef. The boycott was successful in cutting demand and stemming price increases for a short time. With this success, however, the interest group dissolved. It did not reform when meat prices again jumped some six months later.

In contrast to individual and special interest groups, the organisation relies upon a mix of resources and ideologies. As a legal entity in can make and enforce contracts. Via specialization it can control resources needed by other organisations. It need not be concerned about complete consensus on every issue. Resources can be substituted for ideology to maintain control over individuals. Success does not threaten survival but adds resources for growth and development. Thus, organisations are the most important units in the specific environment of other organisations.

To a large extent, then, the important units in the specific environment of an organisation consist of organisations it must relay upon for growth and development. Suppliers or raw materials, financial institutions, unions, government agencies, and competitors are important for most organisations. Occasionally, individuals and special interest groups are important enough to become a part of the enacted environment. Most, however, have used a strategy of operating through government agencies, which then become the relevant units of the enacted environment.

Assessing the specific enviornment of organisations

Three variables appear to be particularly important in analyzing the impact of the specific environment on organisations. These are: (1) the degree of inter-dependence; (2) the extent of uncertainty; and (3) the opportunities for growth and development. Here, we look at each of these.

Interdependence, power, and reliance

When an organisation establishes its domain it automatically becomes more reliant upon some organisations than others. Via exchange, organisations attempt to grow, develop, and, in

Thompson's words, manage their domains. The degree of interdependence of one organisation upon another not only defines the outer boundaries of the specific environment, it also charts the relative importance of various organisations.

We have chosen the term interdependence to highlight the reciprocal nature of exchanges among organisations. If A and B are interdependent, both have some degree of clout over the other. The pattern of dependence in the specific environment appears to have two dimensions. First, to what extent is the focal organisation more dependent upon others than they are upon it? That is, what is the relative power of the organisation? Two, how interdependent are the members of the specific environment upon one an other? Even a powerful system may be forced to adapt if all the weaker units demand it. Perhaps a variation of an Aesop fable will illustrate interdependence.

The lion and the fox agreed to cooperate in the hunt. The fox would chase the game and the lion would come in for an easy kill. Together they killed in one day what each could do alone in a week. When dividing the spoils the fox wisely asked the lion for a fair share. The lion gave the fox more than the fox could have killed along, but still a very small share. The analogy to organisations is clear. The benefits from exchange need not be equivalent. If both parties benefit from the exchange, it is likely the relationship will be voluntarily maintained.

The Relative Power of an Organisation. We said the relative power of an organisation vis-a vis its specific environment is the first aspect of interdependence. But what is the overall pattern of reciprocation? Is the organisation the fox or the lion? The greater the reliance of the organisation upon others, the more responsive the organisation must be to environmental alterations. Why? The organisation receives comparatively less return for its efforts. Thus, it has comparatively little margin for error. Slight changes can eliminate the benefits from exchanges. The organisation has comparatively fewer internal resources to initiate new exchange relationships. Note, however, it's still better off with the exchanges than without them.

The pattern of dependence is rarely the same for goals, output, property, technology, structure, and members. Some of these internal elements must be obtained from a single source. As economic theory clearly shows, the monopolist has a more favorable exchange condition. For instance, if a union controls the labor supply, it can bargain for higher wages, fringe benefits, and worker prerogatives than would be found in a free labor market. It tilts the exchange in favor of the union.

However, unfavorable exchange situations can be eased or altered. To continue our example of the union, assume the organisation has developed a favorable exchange relationship with distributors. To some extent higher wages can be passed on to these units which in turn are likely to pass them on to individual consumers. This directly eliminates the unfavorable exchange relationship.

An indirect way to reduce dependence might be through the use of other external forces. Assume a business corporation faces the same union as before, but may be unable to pass on extra costs. In previous negotiations the corporation has already bargained away the right to promote employees on the basis of performance. Seniority determines progression. The business might ask the Equal Employment Opportunity Commission to rule that seniority was inherently discriminatory. Seniority reflects previous patterns of discrimination against females and minorities. Given such a ruling, the business has some additional leverage over the union. The seniority system is now bargaining issue.

As these examples show, dependence is not static. Several entities may be involved to determine the degree of dependence on outside groups.

Domain Protection and Interdependence. We think organisations will seek areas where favorable exchange relationships are more likely and tend to expand their domain into areas they can dominate. They may even help develop new organisations that will offset the power of an important unit in the specific environment. Thompson argues that such efforts stem from the organisation's desire to protect its "technical core." This means that the organisation will attempt to protect the major processes it uses to produce its products and services. Following Thompson's general notion we expect that an organisation will be particularly vehement in protecting its fixed investment. Protection of an organisation's fixed investment is needed to ensure long-term survival.

To produce the outputs needed, an organisation must often invest in capital equipment, long-term employment contracts, and the like. For instance, producing automobiles requires a huge long-run commitment of resources in machinery and equipment. Only minor shifts from the existing technology are possible in the short run. Major alterations would threaten the existence of the system. This rigidity results primarily from specialization. Specialization is both the organisation's major strength and weakness. It's basis for exchanges with members in the specific environment. But the rigidity inherent in specialization means an organisation must protect its long-term investments. Conversely, if control over less critical elements is challenged, its survival may not be directly threatened. It can move out of one area and seek favorable exchange relationships in others.

These arguments again reveal the critical importance of suppliers, distributors, and government agencies. Suppliers and distributors are needed to protect internal operations. Government agencies can preempt the jurisdiction of an organisation over elements needed to maintain its central technology. A complementary argument is that competitors are a critical feature of the specific environment. They also compete for suppliers and distributors and seek to protect their investments. It's no wonder, then, that organisations attempt to dilute the impact of these important members of the specific environment.This is done by securing several sources of supply, developing numerous distributors, pitting one governmental agency against another wherever possible, and in some cases, trying to expand their domain.

Interdependence within the Specific Environment. Let's return to the story of the lion and the fox to illustrate another aspect of interdependence. The arrangement between the fox and the lion was so successful that the fox convinced the lion to expand and make the same arrangement with twelve foxes. The kill rate was amazing.The arrangement was so efficient that game started to disappear. After a particularly poor day's hunt the foxes demanded and got a larger share of the spoils.

Collective action is not always needed to alter the policies or internal operations of a more powerful and autonomous organisation. If each demanded a large share separately, the lion might still have trouble. While busy with one fox, another could take more. In much the same fashion, when an organisation faces an interdependent set of organisations in the specific environment, it must often succumb to the desires of less powerful and less autonomous units. Thus, organisations seek a specific environment where the members are not interdependent. It is expected that interdependence among members of the specific environment has much the same impact on an organisation as the degree of reliance upon one external unit. The greater the interdependence, the greater the probability that the organisation will: (a) seek to alter its domain; (b) become more responsive to pressures from members in the specific environment; (c) derive less from exchanges with other organisations; and (d) spend more effort on monitoring external conditions.

The Impact of Interdependence on Organisations. We have already covered some kinds of organisational response to interdependence. here, as in the Measurement Module, we will distinguish between objective and perceptual measures of interdependence. Let's look at a few studies that have been done about the effect of this on organisational operations and outcome.

In a well-known and often criticized study, Aiken and Hage studied interdependence among health and welfare agencies, as measured by the number of joint programs. Interdependence was positively associated with the degree of professional activity by members, the degree of specialization, the number of new innovative programs, as well as the amount of coordinative activities such as committee meetings.

In another sample of health-related organisations, Paulson found much the same as Aiken and Hage. But his data raise an interesting question of casualty. Most researchers assume that environmental conditions lead to alterations in the internal structure and operations of organisations. Paulson's data, however, suggested that this pattern of causation might be quite the opposite. Namely, a more sophisticated structure leads to greater interdependence. This shouldn't be too surprising if we assume that organisations seek a favorable domain and establish mechanisms to accomplish control. It may very well be that the structure needed to interface with other organisation is established before detailed arrangements, like joint programs, are perfected. There maybe a process of mutual adjustment over time. That is, environmental interdependence is altered by and alters organisational structure. We will continue to treat the major causation chain as moving from environmental conditions to organisational structure and operations. This is the most popular view. But you should be aware of the conflicting evidence. At any rate, interdependence has some influence on an organisation and its members, when measured "objectively."

Studies relying upon executive perceptions of interdependence also show it is an important factor for organisations. Even though top managers may not accurately perceive the degree of interdependence, they act on their perceptions. When top managers see more interdependence they tend to centralize decision making. Specialized units may be formed to meet dependence on powerful units in the specific environment. Greater reliance on outsiders has also been associated with an ideological shift toward the dominant values of more powerful external systems. Freeman shows that reliance upon other units is associated with greater leadership activity on the part of unit heads, particularly in regard to developing more external contacts.

Thus, results for both objective and perceptual measures seem to be consistent. Interdependence is related to organisational structure and operations as well as short-term effectiveness. However, most of the empirical investigations are with small nonprofit organisations and center on "cooperation" as desirable among organisations. To include larger scale organisations and profit-seeking systems we must move to indirect measures of specific environment interdependence. Here the data are somewhat less clear. But the support the general notion that interdependence increases he complexity of an organisations' structure, reduces the perceived autonomy of managers, and is positively related to short-term profitability. The overall impact on long-term survival and growth still awaits empirical investigation.

In sum, interdependence is an important variable in assessing the specific environment of an organisation. yet it is not only important factor. Uncertainty in the specific environment has also been related to internal operations and effectiveness. So let's look at this variable.

Uncertainty in the specific environment

While there are many different views of environmental uncertainty, it is easiest to see in therm of interrelated dimensions: disparity and volatility. We will discuss each of these factors and their association with effectiveness and internal operations.

Disparity. The first aspect of uncertainty in the specific environment of an organisation is called disparity We have shown that an organisation deals with several other organisations. These outside organisations constitute the core of the specific environment. As the number of types of these external organisations increases, disparity increases. These organisations may be different in many ways. An analysis of key organisational characteristics and of interdependence suggests that differences in goals, outputs, technology, structure, size, and employees are important.

Disparity increases the risk for an organisation. It does this in several different ways. The more varied the members, the greater the conflict potential. As the membership of the specific environment becomes more varied, the probability of instability also increases. Organisations face similar pressures from the general environment. When membership becomes more varied, however, the chances of unified pressures from the general environment decline rapidly. The ability of an organisation to influence the specific environment also appears to deçline as disparity of the environment increases. Furthermore, greater disparity also reduces the ability of decision makers to accurately predict the actions of outside units. Estimates for one outside organisation do not apply to others.

We should note that such disparity is a two-way street. While it increase risk, it also increases the autonomy executives see in their jobs. At the same time the organisation has less influence over oversiders, outsiders also have less control over the organisation.

There are comparatively few empirical studies showing the association of disparity and organisational processes or outcomes. Yet systems analysts have given disparity a key role in their analyses of organisations. Ashby among others, argues that greater disparity in external factors should be matched with greater variability internal to the organisation. Organisations that follow this "law of requisite variety" are expected to have higher survival potential. At least one empirical analysis suggests that organisations that follow this "law" are more likely to reach their output goals.

Volatility. Many organisations find it particularly difficulty to cope with changes in trends. In panel A, we find little volatility even though there is considerable change. Here there is little uncertainty. The trend is relatively constant. In panel B there is fluctuation and directional instability; but we can still predict the cycle of change. Here, the organisations faces some uncertainty. This is due to the lack of directional stability. Yet a trend is still present. In panel C the velocity, acceleration, and directional stability all appear random. Here the organisation faces considerable uncertainty. There appears to be no trend. In our terms the specific environment would be volatile.

Volatility is the enemy of all organisations. It can upset established patterns of control and interdependence. It reduces the value of the organisation's resources and signals a potential shift in the value of its ideology. Existing patterns of specialization and current outputs may no longer be appropriate.

Organisational and Managerial Responses to Uncertainty. Organisations appear to anticipate the value of future outcomes from current inputs, and discount for risk. Many develop specialized units to cope with uncertainty, which can be linked to specific external units. Environmental uncertainty appears to paralyze some decision makers. When it appears that an organisation no longer controls its fate, decision makers often attempt to build slack to buffer dysfunctional changes.

When first formed, the Equal Employment Opportunity Commission frequently changed guidelines for minority hiring procedures. Many firms responded with centralized affirmative action units. You can imagine what happened.The EEOC issued new regulations for minority hiring that were to be implemented immediately. Regulations were filled with bureaucratic jargon the few could understand, and the EEOC kept reinterpreting the standards. The solution: put someone in charge of the minority relations program. That person can figure out what the EEOC really wants. The head of the new Minority Relations Office obviously needed a staff to cope with the ever changing demands of the EEOC. The Minority Relations Office also needed the support of the top brass for this important effort. Thus, the unit was placed near the top of the organisational hierarchy.

But was this typical response successful? It might be for the derived goal of hiring minority workers. But it might not be in regard to other goals. Several studies have found that firms that resisted the temptation to develop specialized units in the face of greater volatility had higher performance ratings on outputs, which could be directly linked with the mission of the system. In slightly different terms, firms that desire greater overall success must, we think, resist the temptation of overstructuring in the face of environmental volatility. They should not develop specialized bureaus, departments, and agencies with a later increase in the number of rules, policies, and procedures. Instead, the organisation should rely more upon the informal organisation.

Part of the reason for this suggestion is that managers operate in the face of perceptual as well as objective uncertainty. These presumptions influence how they operate. Specifically, fewer good decisions are made by individuals as uncertainty increase. Managers move to a form of decision making where they consult more with each other they abandon rigid decision rules and circumvent the formal relationships dictated by the bureaucracy. Under high risk, then, the individual who has the relevant information becomes important and a key in the decision-making process. Organisations become more flexible and less bureaucratic as manager increase their later contacts. Note that the creation of a specialized unit runs counter to managers' attempts to cope with uncertainty. It forms managers to interact when they don't want to.

The amount of perceived uncertainty may also alter the success of a particular leadership style and particular leader behaviors. Nebecker shows that how a leader perceives environmental uncertainty will alter his other views of opportunities for influence. This, in turn, may alter the impact of leadership style. For example, Hunt and Osborn suggest that since uncertainty cuts the discretion or clout of a leader, managers may withdraw from leadership roles. Several other studies show the same disturbing negative effects of perceived environmental uncertainty on individual behavior and group conditions. As a group the studies combining perceptual and objective uncertainty suggest the following: (1) some volatility seen by managers is not directly traceable to the specific environment; it appears to stem from a combination of personality factors, job experience, and internal organisational conditions; (2) perceived uncertainty appears to foster more informal relations among managers; but such relations may be virtually eliminated if the organisation becomes more bureaucratic; (3) the tendency of the organisation to bureaucratize in response to uncertainty appears to lower effectiveness; and (4) uncertainty appears to have a small negative impact on effectiveness of the organisation but a larger and more profound negative impact on decision makers. In summary, environmental uncertainly appears quite harmful for bureaucracies that rely heavily on centralized decision making and rigidly adhere to rules.

Interdependence and Uncertainty. We argued earlier that interdependence has a favorable association with organisational performance. We also noted that uncertainly was generally unfavorable. A logical question is what happens when the specific environment is both highly interdependent and uncertain? The combination of high interdependence and high uncertainty is particularly damaging to the organisation. Put a different way, interdependence can be a double-edged sword. Greater dependence is favorable only when the specific environment has low uncertainty.Some analyses suggest that volatility is the chief culprit. The organisation facing a volatile and highly interdependent specific environment can lose control. It can become a tool of outside interests and be unable to change operations to produce viable outputs. How can a organisation cope with the high interdependence, high variability setting?

When two organisations attempt to control the same resources, there appear to be several techniques that can be used to resolve the conflict. The dispute may be resolved by custom, dominant values, or law. The legal technique is the most expensive and restrictive. We argue it is more likely to be used as the disparity of the specific environment increases. Organisations may also exchange resources, trade existing resources for contested ones, or develop a new ideology that minimizes the conflict. As organisations in the specific setting become more diverse, it is more difficult for any organisation to develop an appropriate medium for exchange or forge a new ideology.

Contesting organisations may agree to disagree, with each claiming a different area of control. For instance, a medical association may share partial control over physicians with hospitals. The association will claim control over how physicians should practice medicine by instructing them in the latest techniques. The hospital will attempt to control physicians by deciding which types of illness it will treat. Since the association and hospitals share similar domains, conflict is not typically extensive.

But now add a quite divergent group to the specific environment of the hospital. Assume it is owned by a religious order. Now the hospital must systematically consider how spiritual concerns will or will not constrain physicians. Again, greater disparity increases the difficulty in resolving conflict with this technique.

Another technique is merger. Here one organisation merely incorporates another. Again as disparity increases it becomes more difficult to use this technique. The benefits of merger are less the more diverse the merging organisations.

Two other possibilities are virtually eliminated by high interdependence. Remember, high interdependence means the organisation must find some way of resolving domain conflict. One, they cannot withdraw without losing power. Two, they can't eliminate the other organisation without suffering the consequences. Thus, where there is considerable disparity among organisations in a specific environment, resolving domain disputes among highly interrelated organisations becomes move difficult and costly. Yet the organisation can still have some control over its fate.

Development in the specific environment

Almost unrecognized in the current literature is the resource base of organisations comprising the specific environment. The composition of the specific environment changes slowly over time. An organisation is typically committed to an ideology and a whole series of long-term investments. Thus, an organisation is stuck with many units in the specific environment. It may be associated with a series of powerful organisations that are growing and contain large reserves of resources. Conversely, an organisation may be interacting wit a series of weak, declining organisations. Does it make a difference? Some data and several theoretical discussions suggest it makes a substantial difference on the outreach activity of the organisation, its internal operations and its annual effectiveness. First, let's briefly look at some different aspects of development. Then we can review the evidence suggesting the importance of development in predicting organisational success.

Development in the specific environment appears to have two dimensions. First, what is the pattern of growth in the specific environment of the organisation? Are the members growing in terms of power, size, technical sophistication, and the like? Or are they on the decline? When an organisation interacts with growing systems there are greater opportunities for domain expansion. Favorable exchange relationships are also more plentiful. Members of the specific environment are less concerned with getting the best exchange than in assuring needed inputs for continued growth. With growth, outsiders are more willing to defer "payment" and accept future assurances. That is, they "bank" some of their excess in other organisations and "invest" resources in new exchange relationships with long-term payoffs.

Quite the opposite seems true fro systems experiencing a decline. They cut "investment" in other organisations. They become very concerned with immediate returns. They may attempt to "borrow" from members of the specific environment, placing a strain on existing exchange relationships. For instance, outsiders with excess labor are less likely to let an organisation perform specialized services. They will attempt to use their excess labor even though outsiders could do a better and more efficient job

At the very time outsiders may need cooperative relationships to conserve resources and more efficiently use existing capacity, such efforts are not undertaken. Why? Co-operation among organisations primarily involves long-term payoffs after a period of expensive "investment."

The second aspect of development is somewhat more complex since it involves the notion of the interorganisational set. An interorganisational set is a collection of organisations interrelated either directly via exchange relationship or via the production and distribution of a given product or service. The notion of industry is very similar to that of the interorganisational set. It is an example of a set based on the production and distribution of a given product or service. Those familiar with market channels will not that a channel of distribution is another type of interorganisational set.

What is the relative power of the members of the organisational set(s) that an organisation is a part of? If the set is large and powerful, members of the set are likely to face a more favorable environment. Large organisations facing less competition are more likely to have excess resources they can divert toward their long-term growth and survival. They are likely to be more specialized and maintain a cadre of technical experts. Since organisations rely upon other organisations, some of these excess resources can be diverted to outsiders. For instance, major soda-extract companies have helped local bottlers fight restrictions on disposable containers. They work with bottlers on technical matters and, most of all, supplement local advertising. They will help perform market studies, lobby for the industry, and the like. Similarly, some critics of the auto industry have argued that the major manufacturers are more interested in the dealers that in consumers.

Organisational and Managerial Responses to Development. The power of the set does not without a price. Even argues that it comes at the expense of autonomy. Each organisation must anticipate the impact of its decisions on a whole series of external units. For instance, how do you price a product in an oligopolistic industry? You must consider the pricing strategy of competitors and the impact of the pricing strategy on the channel of distribution. The organisational set and its members are less likely to innovate and anticipate broader social changes as the control and power of the set increase. As Selznick noted, the major units of the set appear to exchange and modify their goals and ideology over time until there is a high degree of domain consensus. Critics of federal regulatory agencies have noted a similar process. Major corporations and government agencies have become an inter-organisational set with a common set of goals and compatible ideologies.

Development may have its greatest direct impact on the performance of an organisation and its managers. Just as powerful organisations may tip the balance of exchange in their favor, so can powerful organisational sets. They are in a position to lobby for favorable governmental action including protectionist legislation, direct subsidies, and price controls. By controlling the output of an important good or service they may increase its prices to the society much as the Organisation of Petroleum Exporting Countries has done with crude oil. For governmental units, development also has some very subtle overtones. Via cooperative action, government agencies can legitimize each other so that more funds flow into a given problem area. For instance, state universities operating together can help promote the importance of a college degree regardless of which institution grants the diploma. But one university does not publicly criticize another much as one physician does not testy against a colleague. It's bad for the set. Thus, both resources and performance distortion can occur when the set is growing. However, as a member of the set both the organisation and its managers benefit.

To the extent that resources flow into an organisation as a result of membership in a strong interorganisational set, managers have more resources to work with. Mistakes can be covered with abundant resources. Managers can take credit for growth. They can attract more qualified personnel, reward even marginal performers, and more easily maintain both high satisfaction and performance. However, when the efficiency crunch comes, as it did in education and aerospace, the opposite occurs. Organisations are not given credit for their outputs. Managers can't get the resources they need to maintain high performance and satisfaction. The brightest and the best move on to other areas; the set has problems attracting new blood. And successful administrators are deemed inadequate.

This second aspect of development is the least researched and most controversial. It can be supported by a number f theoretical articles. But we are not aware of any empirical studies relating the power of the interoganizational set to the internal operations or effectiveness of organisations. Thus you should view this aspect of development caution.

2 The Ecology of Organisations

To *create* and *renew* organisations for the process of innovation—these are the specialized jobs of managers in such people-systems. And since no system can be better than its parts, managers must find ways of maintaining and improving the excellence of all their people for their specialized and cooperative roles in the innovation process.

But while it is necessary to renew individuals, this alone is not sufficient to ensure a viable, ever-growing organisation. The manager also must help his organisation to renew its purpose, structure, and technological content. It is not enough to understand the systems nature of innovation and organisations. We must delve more deeply into the *nature* of people-systems. Though they are systems, *they are not machines*!

The organisation as an organism

Throughout this book, we have emphasized the *creative, living* nature of organisations, their "organic" behavior. And we have also said that people-systems become more complex as they grow later. Indeed, the same is true of a technological system. the bigger any kind of system gets, the more complex it must become. It might be a railroad network, a national telephone system, or a school system—but bigness and complexity always go together for survival.

If any system is also to grow in *capability* as it gets bigger, if it is to avoid getting old and arthritic, something has to be happening inside it. Two things in fact: As the specializations of the system multiply, they have to keep improving, and the *couplings* between those specialized parts *also* must improve. Herbert Spencer recognized this long ago when he drew an analogy between biological and social systems: "A social organism is like an individual organism in these essential traits: that it grows; that while growing it becomes more complex; that in both cases there is increasing integration...accompanied by increasing heterogeneity..."

Growth in specialization and coupling, and hence in complexity, leads to higher capability. And this is where managers are needed. Once an organisation is created, the manager's continuing job is to help it to keep growing in capability, to help it in self-renewal. Saying it in a new way, the manager's job is "the innovation of innovation." His responsibility is the creation and adaptive change—in purpose, content, and structure—of his people-system.

The systems approach and its model of the innovative process contain this concept of improvement through ever-more-complex iterations. And since every system is a specialized part of a larger system, this view of the manager's job holds for every manager, at all levels in an organisation, from the lower ranks right up to the presidency. The only difference from level to level is in the breadth of purpose and the complexity of content, structure, and environment.

Toward an ecological viewpoint

Every manager must remember that the *components* of his system are living creative *people*, each with his own hierarchy of human needs and abilities. The manager must not try to "program" this machine, for it is not really a machine at all. It is not rigid in content or structure, blindly following a fixed purpose. Rather, it is a *being*, composed of living interacting parts. It is a living organism which can learn, change itself, and grow in its changing world.

How then is the manager's job different from the job of the system engineer? The system engineer is dealing with an *inanimate*

system, but the manager is dealing with a *living* system. It is true, the manager should design "in the mood of a social-systems engineer." And if he must not program a people-system as he would an inanimate system, what then is his role?

We believe that he must also be an *agent of change-a mutation selector*! Through his understanding of the innovation process, he can stimulate, select, and reinforce those particular responses of the organism itself which increase its capability for purposive innovation. He can become the "Maxwell Demon of mutation"-the demon described in the Foreword-and in this role he can increase the probability that his organism will succeed adaptively in its environment. In fact, he can go one better on nature's process of evolution, in which only a few of the many random mutations survive.

Many times when we wrestling with a problem, an analogy helps me to change my viewpoint and to use the wisdom of others. Applied with caution, analogy provided a new model, affords a new way of seeing things, and frequently leads to important questions that you had not thought of before. We have already used the analogies of the programmer, the scientist, and the systems engineer to describe the manager's role. Each time we have gained broader understanding-and each time we have seen a new dimension of the manager's role. Now we want to change our viewpoint once again and see the manager as the "Innovator of Innovation."

This viewpoint is too new to me to assure me of its wide applicability. But all we ask of a new viewpoint and model is simply that it be *useful*-to posing new questions that our old model ignored, or asking old questions in a new way. Indeed, that is all any scientist asks of a new viewpoint. It need not be ultimate truth; it need only be useful in enlarging his range of questions and critical experiments, and it should not clash with the useful parts of older models.

We have already been sneaking in some of the

language of the new viewpoint. It is the language of "biological ecology," the new inter-disciplinary science devoted to understanding how living organisms adapt to their environment. It was in this context that we spoke of the manager as the *agent of change*," as the Maxwell Demon for adaptive mutations.

And if the concepts of ecology help us to ask new questions about the internal and external workings of our people system-how it makes synapses between need and possibility; how it chooses among alternate technologies; hoOw it responds to threat or opportunity; and how it changes purpose, content, and structure for growth-if it opens these areas for fresh inquiry, it will be useful. We do not need all the detailed concepts of ecology. In fact, it is not desirable to push an analogy too far; there are always important differences in detail. For our purpose, which is to suggest new questions, we need only a few key ideas and the simplest of models.

As we said, ecology is concerned with the interactions between living organisms, or "species"' and their environment. The environment is made up of the physical nonliving world and other living species. Different species group together in their environment to form "communities." Each species can be differentiated by its particular function, content, and structure. The concept of a "major community" is an intriguing one. It is an assemblage of different species or communities and their physical environment, so interacting that all are *symbiotic*: They learn to live together in their environment in a self-adjusting, complementary manner. This is an important point when we think about organisational survival, as we shall soon see. The total environment resulting from living species and physical effects is called an "ecosystem."

With these elemental ideas and terms, we can construct a model of a species or community in its ecosystem, as shown in Figure. Note the internal and external forces that act to change the purpose, content, and structure of the species or community. Some of these forces come from the ecosystem; we formerly thought of them as just inputs to be processed by the organism. They can be purely physical, from the nonliving environment, or biological, from the other living species in the major community. Other forces come from the activity of the species itself, from its own specialized and integrated activities. They, too, can be physical or biological.

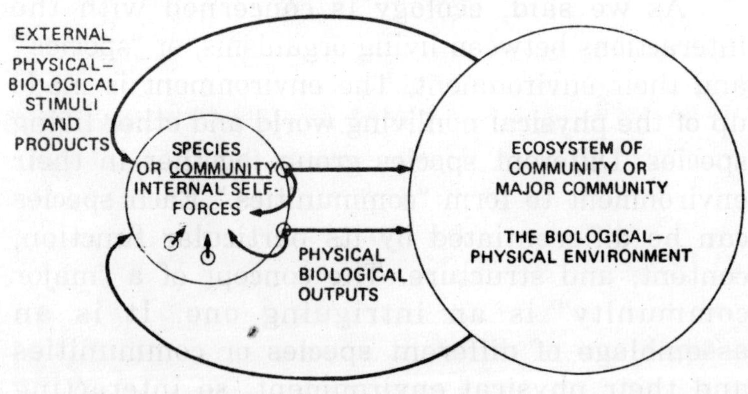

Biological ecology

For the species or community to exist symbiotically in its ecosystem—and, with others, form a major community-it must be able to adapt to all the forces of change, whether these forces are generated within itself or come from its ecosystem. All the species in a community try to survive and grow by developing their specialized abilities to use certain relevant inputs from their ecosystem. And each species generates unique functions and outputs that must be useful to its ecosystem. Thus, each species differs from all others, and each community from other communities, by its particular purpose, content, and structure. Taken together, these characteristics define the unique identity of a species or community. This is how it relates to its environment.

Let us apply this model and its concepts to our problem. Our various specialists correspond to species. Grouped together in their corporation environment, they form a community. Each corporation is characterized by its particular purpose, content, and structure.

Now let us immerse such a corporation into its ecosystem: its physical world and all the other specialized enterprises of its major community. Let us look at the interrelationships between them. They match pretty well in many respects.

But something new has been added! Not only does the ecosystem provide the inputs-capital, knowledge. and resources- to be processed into useful outputs, but these stimuli also act as *forces* for adaptive *change* in the organism itself. Further, the activities of the community, both the internal specialized "products" and the total "outputs," act as additional change-forces. Looking at things in this new way, we see that the community,m or corporation, does more than simply produce fixed outputs that are useful to itself and its ecosystem. *Equally important, it tries to improve its survival through adaptive change of its purpose, content, and structure.*

Remember, in the systems-engineering model, these properties were *fixed*. When you thought of the manager's job in terms of that model, he was the designer or the operator of a machine, an *inorganic* system. But now, we can see things differently; We see living species *themselves* responding adaptively to the internal and external forces of change.

Now we have a new perspective on the manager's role. He must be alert and sensitive to changes both in his organism and its ecosystem as they interact. He will want to stimulate some of these changes himself, and to reinforce or discourage others generated by his living organism. In all cases, he wants to encourage those changes in purpose, content, and structure which will contribute most to the long term survival and growth of his system. Now he is acting as the Maxwell Demon for the "hot ideas" that produce the most adaptive mutations.

For example, as markets and knowledge change, new needs and opportunities arise. Of all

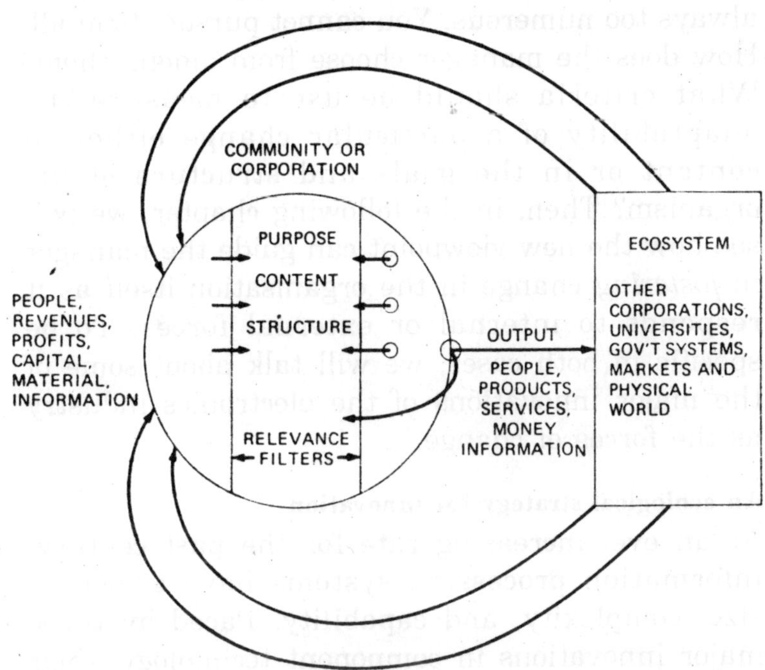

The ecology of organisations

the possible combinations of problems and solutions dreamed up by creative people, the Demon Manager wants to select and support those which are most relevant and cost-effective to his long-term mission. Or his living organism, will even try to *change itself*, in response to an important external innovation. Now we are getting somewhere! Now we are getting self-renewal, renewal of the organisation. All the living parts of the organisation are parts of that renewal process: Everyone is generating new ideas; everyone has a piece of the action. And the manager wants to stack the deck for winning!

But the new ideas, the new opportunities, are always too numerous. You cannot pursue them all. How does the manager choose from among them? What criteria should be use to measure the adaptability of a particular change either in content or in the goals and structure of his organism? Then, in the following chapter, we will see how the new viewpoint can guide the manager in *fostering* change in the organisation itself as it responds to internal or external forces. To be specific in both cases, we will talk about some of the major innovations of the electronics industry as the forces of change.

An ecological strategy for innovation

At an ever-increasing rate for the past century, information processing systems have grown in size, complexity, and capability. Paced by three major innovations in component technology, their change is being accelerated by a fourth, that of integrated electronics.

In those earlier eras, tactical choices for innovation were simple to make. The number of potential markets and technologies was limited. New developments complemented, rather than competed with , the old. Each was needed to build a larger system capability. Moreover, the time interval between choices was long enough to ensure a rewarding return on investment in innovation.

But in the past two decades the number of technologies possible for innovation has grown rapidly. And the new technologies are much more competitive with each other and with the old. All this increases the possibility, and the *risk,* that a technology will become obsolete before its innovation is complete and before a return can be made on its investment. Today there are more opportunities to lose your shirt than to make killing. Short-term tactics, without long-term goals and strategies, *can* be disastrous.

To make sound tactical choices, each enterprise must have a clear view of its markets and resources. Only then can the enterprise determine the particular mix of cost, performance, and reliability objectives for its innovations. But these classical measures of cost-effectiveness are no longer enough to ensure economic survival. We also must ask about the potential *longevity* of a technology. Can it survive the changes that are sure to come in knowledge and markets? *Is it adaptive*? This is a *new* strategic question

In a way, a technology is a system. It is composed of specialized materials and phenomena that interact to produce useful functions. Like organisms, technologies can be viewed as species seeking survival and growth in a changing ecosystem of relevant science, different technologies, and competing markets. To understand this new requirement for adaptability, let us review the past cycles of electric component innovation. Many of our older technologies are still vigorous today. Perhaps we can identify the essential measures of their adaptability. Hopefully, we can use this understanding to gauge the innovative lifetime of old and new technologies

The adaptability of component technologies. The first era of electrical-information systems depended critically upon electromechanical relays and telephones. Together with resistors, capacitors, inductors, and batteries, they supplied the functions essential to begin telegraphy and telephony in the nineteenth century. While telegraphy could span thousands of miles, telephony, with its weaker voice signals, was limited to a few hundred miles. Longer distances could be covered. but the only amplifiers for the waning voice currents were electromechanical. They were bulky and costly and wasted large amounts of power. It was their electromechanical nature that set limits to the functions they could perform, and thus prevented the full development of communications at about the turn of the century.

The second era of component innovation was sparked in 1906 by Lee De Forest's invention of the triode vacuum tube. Here was an invention that opened up new opportunities for innovation. New *electronic* amplifiers and systems could now be developed, and these would be far superior in performance, cost, and use of power. By 1914, through research, development, and manufacture, the electron tube had established its superiority in performance and its adequacy in reliability, to the point that it made possible the first United States transcontinental telephone service. During the next several years electron tubes continued to get better. Their performance improved sharply. They became increasingly reliable. And all the while, their cost kept going down. Now it became possible to send many telephone and telegraph messages at a time over a single radio channel or pair of wires.

But those early tubes did not displace the relays. Yes, they could perform digital functions much faster than relays. Yes, they could perform digital functions much faster than relays could, but tubes were more expensive and less reliable than relays. So the relay was destined to be around for a good long while. As a matter of fact, the real significance of this second ear of innovation, sparked by the invention of the vacuum tube, was that it caused a great expansion of the communications market. More telephones were used, larger switching systems were needed to interconnect them, and this created new demands for both vacuum tubes *and* relays.

At the same time, as tube technology improved, it created new markets for still other kinds of electric systems. Broadcast radio and home recording spawned a vigorous new consumer market.

Over some 40 years, electron tubes continued to improve and new types of tubes continued to be developed. Once again, the newer technology complemented the old. Microwave tubes, such as klystrons, magnetrons, and travelling wave tubes, greatly expanded the message carrying ability of transmission media, and new electrooptical functions were added with cathode-ray display and camera tubes. Now we are into the thirties and forties. And as we said, these new component innovations did not displace the older technologies; they supplemented them. As each component innovation was added, systems capability grew. And it kept going for years. After World War II, the consumer market received another big boost from television. Military markets grew rapidly. Tube computers opened a new industrial market. Each of these market expansions was really based on the same basic technology, going back to the 1906 De Forest triode. The extensions of this technology made possible more complex systems requiring hundred, thousand, and sometimes tens of thousand of tubes, passive components, and, yes, relays. In fact, relays and passive components had growth curves that looked as healthy as the growth curve for tubes. Because of the slow pace of change and the complementary nature of component technologies during the forty years of the first two eras, the return on their innovation was large. You could lose your shirt in those days, but it was harder, it took longer, and the risks were not nearly so great.

However, these apparent virtues cloaked some serious limitations. Each component technology was highly specialized. Each relied on different physical phenomena, material-systems, and processes of manufacture. As a result, these technologies differed widely in their intrinsic limits of size, power, and speed. They also differed in their cost and reliability. All were inefficient users of power. All were large and bulky, and their mechanical and chemical fragility led to high maintenance expenses. These limitations and their differences became high economic barriers to further growth in the size, complexity, and capability of electronic systems.

Indeed, it was the recognition of these barriers that led to the third era, the era of transistor technology beginning in 1948. Here was a new technology of great power. In fact, it was so high in versatility and cost-effectiveness that not much time would pass before transistors were competing with, and even surpassing, almost all the older technologies. In just 20 years, transistor technology improved enormously in performance, cost, and reliability-for both analogue and digital functions. As a result, all electronics markets were greatly stimulated.

Since the early fifties, the military and industrial parts have grown at a faster rate than the consumer market. This has resulted in a corresponding growth rate for semiconductor components, that is, transistors and their progeny. In fact, it is almost three times the rate for tubes. Let us now examine semiconductor technology from the viewpoint of adaptability. The physical phenomena of semiconductor components are themselves highly adaptable. They have proved their versatility for a wide range of electric-signal processing, for electric signals in either digital or analogue form. Moreover, semiconductor devices can provide electroacoustical and electrooptical signal-processing functions as well. Thus, within a single class of compatible electronic materials, semiconductors, we are able to achieve most of the complementary functions needed to provide complete capability in processing information of all kinds. Formerly, as you remember, we needed many different technologies, and they did not fit so well together in size, power, cost, or reliability. On the other hand, to achieve this compatibility, and the economic advantages that the new semiconductor science offered. We had to innovate a great deal in the materials and processes of semiconductor devices. And therein lies the tale of the great ferment that has stirred the semiconductor era.

The first invention of this era, the "point-contact germanium transistor," was limited in all three measures of effectiveness: It did not perform well; it cost too much; and it lacked reliability. This first transistor was also difficult to understand in detail and, as a result, was not used very long. But a second kind of structure was soon developed. Called a "grown-junction transistor," it could be made also in silicon, a material superior to germanium for high-temperature and high-power applications. Because of their superior performance and reliability, grown-junction transistors were the first stimulants to real market development. Because we could apply science to their development, we were able to extend rapidly the performances and reliability of both germanium and silicon devices. Nevertheless, grown-junction technology did not last very long either, because a newer technology soon came along, alloy-junction technology. And although it was used only for germanium, the lower cost and superior switching performance of alloy transistors swept them into command of the consumer radio and computer markets.

By the late fifties, alloy germanium transistors had about reached the limitations of our understanding and control of their processes. Their cost was down to about the lowest limit for devices which had to be made one at a time. Their reliability was very high, but they were limited to low temperature and low power, because the alloy process worked well only with germanium. Moreover, their signal-processing speeds were still much lower than desired, because of intrinsic limitations of the alloy structure.

But already, in 1954, new high-precision processes of oxide masking and diffusion were demonstrated for silicon as well as germanium. So again, a materials technology did not last very long: in just a few years, diffusion technology surpassed alloy technology in both performance and reliability. And it had the potential for lower cost because it permitted batch fabrication of thousands of devices at one time on a single slice of semiconductor, except for the final few *one-at-a-time* processes. Equally important, diffusion technology was adaptive to different materials, device structures, and markets. With one easy addition of new refinements, namely, epitaxial and planar techniques, diffusion technology proved its adaptability to new knowledge. And new functions and markets grew once again.

Thus, until the introduction of batch diffusion, the innovative life for each new transistor technology was short: but a few years. The saving grace came from industry rapid exploitation of each advance and the correspondingly fast growth of both old and new markets. In just a few years, batch diffusion was able to push discrete transistors close to their intrinsic in cost, performance, and reliability.

As a result, the cost of diffused transistors dropped precipitously. As we said, thousands of identical transistors are fabricated at one time per slice of semiconductor before they have to be finally cut apart, terminated, and capsulated one at a time. The cost, therefore, approaches a minimum, since it costs a few cents for an operator just to pick up a single item without doing much to it. In fact, it now costs as much, or more, for the operator to pick up and install a transistor into a piece of equipment as it costs to make the transistor in the first place. Moreover, the chance of one of these transistors failing became so small-a few failures per billion device hours-that the cost of measuring and ensuring such low failure rates was *also* exceeding their cost of fabrication. Finally, performance had also been increasingly by these same factors of 10, well into the range of microwave transmission and billionth-of-a-second switching speeds. It, too, was approaching a limit set by the *size of the discrete* components and their interconnections.

So what was the problem? Or had electronics finally reached a kind of Shangrila ? After all, the things that once cost dollars to produce were now being made for a few dimes each-any they were superior in every way. How could you get much better than that ? Let me say that if there were people around who enjoyed complacency in the mid 1950s, they did not enjoy it for long-for still another wave of innovation was about to break, and when it did, there was lots of little pieces to be picked up. We never did say that innovation was easy!

The new wave was necessary in order to break the barrier of discrete planar transistors-what we like to call the "one-at-a-time" barrier. These limitations of plannar transistors were not due to the physics or to batch diffusion technology; both the physics and batch diffusion are still with us today, and going strong. And these planar transistors were indeed very good devices by any measure. But we were still insisting that they be finished as *discrete* elements-to provide maximum flexibility in their application to many different systems. Even though with batch diffusion we could make thousands at one time in a single slice of silicon, we still had to separate, terminate, protect, test, and assemble them one at a time! And it was these one-at-a-time operations that set limits to the cost, performance, and reliability of systems made of such discrete elements.

Many of us could see these limitations in the late fifties; in fact, the opportunity for breaking through the one-at-a-timebarrier appeared with batch diffusion itself. Remember how it greatly reduced cost over alloy technology-right up to the separation and finishing operations, we processed thousands of identical elements at one time. So we asked; Why made them all alike on one slice? And why separate, terminate, and protect each one only to reassemble them with other elements on a costly one-at-a-time basis? With diffusion, oxide masking, and photolithography, why not make many *circuits* at one time? Why not make integrated circuits"-many at one time in a batch?

In 1956, at Bell Laboratories, Ian Ross developed a simple integrated binary-counter circuit using identical planar transistor elements. In 1958, at Texas Instruments, Jack Kilby developed silicon circuits containing mesa diodes, transistors, and resistors interconnected with individual wire leads. A little later, at Fairchild, Robert Noyce and his coworkers introduced the batch interconnection of planar elements in a silicon chip using evaporated aluminum film conductors for the circuit interconnections. The era of integrated electronics had begun.

Using this technology today, we can batch-fabricate not just transistors, but diodes, resistors, and even capacitors, using the same principles of the good old discrete-elements days, namely, epitaxial growth, oxide masking, photolithography, and diffusion. But now, each element in a slice no longer need be identical with all other elements. Instead, a variety of elements and their interconnections are made as a circuit group. And the entity replicated on the slice is now a circuit, not an element, and we batch-fabricate hundreds of circuits per slice.

The round slice at the upper left of Figure 32 shows todays planar technology for making silicon monolithic circuits. Each of the tiny dots on that slice is a complete circuit. In the successive magnifications, we go from the complete slice to a single circuit in the slice. At the lower right, we see one such circuit, magnified 90x; it contains a number of transistors, diodes, resistors, and their interconnections joined as a circuit-all made *many at one time in the slice*. Each slice contains hundreds of such circuits apart, and finish their fabrication one at a time. The individual termination, capsulation, and testing operations are moved from the element to the circuit level.

Planar silicon circuits give us large improvements in cost and reliability. For digital functions, they excel in performance as well. And the economic barriers that were once at the element level are now moved up to the circuit level-we have climbed one more rung on the ladder of complexity. As a result, planar integrated circuits have been applied rapidly to digital systems. Such as computers. As we write this, in the opening days of the seventies, they constitute the lion's share of industry's total effort on integrated electronics. As shown in Figure 30, annual sales of all kinds of integrated components have been growing at the same prodigious pace as did discrete semiconductors. The steep slope and small time displacement of these growth curves illustrate the new pace of innovation and the difficulty of getting an adequate return on one's investment in innovation.

Up to now. I have described the innovation of three different electronics technologies. Each was stimulated by the limitation of an older technology and the potential of relevant research. The first spiral of electronics innovation started with the invention of the tube and reached its limitations in the form of discrete tubes, relays, and associated passive elements. Each was made one at a time and assembled and wired in a circuit one at a time with hand tools.

The second spiral reached its economic maturity using miniature, but discrete, transistors, diodes, and passive components, still finished and assembled one at a time, but batch-interconnected as a circuit on a printed wiring board.

Finally, the current integrated-electronics technology, still young though vigorous is illustrated by the planar monolithic silicon circuit. Using transistor materials and diffusion processes, it provides us with complex integrated circuits which are completely batch-fabricated except for the termination, capsulation, and test operations. Integrated electronics has already had a major impact on the industry, but it has yet to reach its full maturity. To do so will require new critical choices from among a number of alternate paths for further innovation, what criteria can managers use in making these choices ?

The need for an adaptive integration technology. Today's situation reminds me of the mid-fifties, when alloy transistors were riding so smoothly, but when a few "wave-makers" were looking ahead to the batch technology of diffusion and silicon. Today we see the one-at-a-time economic barrier at the intercircuit level, rather than at the interelement level. And a lot of wave-makers are looking again for ways to crack the new barrier. Where do we go now?

One group says: "If some silicon integration is good, let's have a lot! Let's have large scale integration-let's have LSI!" In LSI, we make a lot of different kinds of circuits and then interconnect them as a system, or at least as a subsystem. And it might appear that we can climb many rungs on the ladder of complexity: The costly one-at-a-time wire terminations and protective cans are moved all the way upto the highest possible systems level, for now we put the maximum amount of a complete *system* on the largest slice of silicon we can make. But we afraid this is not as attractive as it may seem. First, it results in low processing yields. A maximum level of integration implies a maximum number of serial process steps; and the overall yield is the total product of the yields of each step. In other words, if the yield of each step is 0.7 (70 percent) and we need half-a-dozen steps, then our yield is 0.7 x 0.7 x 0.7 x 0.7 x 0.7 x 0.7, or only about 0.11 by the time we are through. This is bad enough, but actually we may need a hundred steps. So even with yields of 95 percent we are in serious trouble-we must do better!Integration also implies a minimum production run. Different systems designers often cannot, and many times will not, use the same LSI design. Since you do not get much cumulative production of a given design. costs never come very far down the "learning curve." and economies of scale become hard to get. Finally, the development of LSI designs requires a maximum of cooperation and risk taking between components and systems specialists; and this is an even tough job of integration-of people. We will have more to say about this in the next chapter.

What we saying is this: This farther one pushes LSI, the less adaptive it becomes-the more specific is its particular design and application. It becomes increasingly costly to adapt it to changing knowledge, technology, or markets. Some innovators, recognizing this, have proposed the use of discretionary wiring-"adaptive wiring"-to match each different LSI slice of silicon to the same or different functions. But this requires costly one-at-a-time finishing operations, different for each slice. To gain adaptability, we have lost high-volume batch fabrication-the old trade off problem again. Remember, it was batch fabrication of identical planar chips which has brought us our large gains. It was the cost of operations on individual planar elements that led us to integration. And remember, batch fabrication can pay off only if there is enough production to benefit from the "learning process." Even in a system whose functions can be supplied by a common silicon slice, the need for good yield and economies of scale from the learning curve requires some partitioning between of scale from the learning curve requires some portioning between identical silicon subsystems.

Equally important, however, is the fact that any single material is always limited in the variety of functions it can perform well. Versatile as silicon is, it does not provide the highly precise stable resistors and capacitors needed for some signal processing functions. Further, it is difficult to intermix different kinds of silicon devices in the same slice, since some of them require different material properties. What is more, new physical phenomena in different materials are forthcoming. When these come, we will want to integrate them with the functions which silicon does well. Thus, at least for now, planar LSI does not provide high-yield total batch fabrication-and is not adaptive to changing technology, different systems, or new phenomena!

Electronics innovators must face it: at different levels in different systems, all systems become hybrid. All must contain interconnected material subsystems, alike or different, for economic or performance reasons. We have come full circle on the upward spiral on innovation, from the thesis of monolithic integration to the antithesis of system portioning into specialized, but batch fabricated and interconnected subsystems.

Measures of adaptability and integrability Today's innovator of electronic systems, therefore, faces major new tactical choices. What strategy or partitioning and integration should guide him? Into exactly which material subsystems should he partition his total system? And how should be interconnect them? He knows that his requirements will depend on his markets, and those markets will change. He knows that his present materials technologies will change with time; and he knows that research will lead to new materials and he knows that research will lead to new materials and functions. Can be select technology for integration that can meet and even use such change, that will not become obsolete before he gets hi bait back? What properties should material subsystems have, to provide simultaneously the benefits of integration and adaptability? To some extent, these properties appear to be in conflict. To make tradeoffs among them, we must understand the essence of each.

The aim of integration is *total* fabrication of *each* material subsystem *and* the hybrid system: dividing the cumulative cost of many process steps by the large number of elements and subsystems processed in each batch. We always want to minimize the number of subsystems and the number of process steps in each. But most importantly, we need *batch fabrication* of *all* process steps for *each* subsystem, ranging from element formation and interconnection to termination and protection. In addition, we need batch assembly and interconnection of the hybrid system. The hybrid yield should average, not multiply, the yields of each subsystem. This says that hybrid assembly and intraconnection should combine only good subsystems without damage.

The aim of adaptability is technical and economic flexibility in partitioning a total system into its similar and different subsystems. To benefit from batch fabrication, we must have sufficient cumulative production of each subsystem to come well down its learning-cost curve. For easy tradeoffs between subsystem costs and hybrid assembly costs, we must have complementary and compatibility between material subsystems. Thus, subsystems must be well matched at their interface in size, topology, and metallurgy, and they should be comparable in cost and reliability. If such requirements are met, the designer can partition his total system optimally with regard to both performance and cost. He also will be able to change his partitioning as the yields of his subsystems technologies improve, as new materials and phenomena appear, and as markets and systems requirements change.

An adaptive strategy for integrated electronics

Today, there are a great and growing number of electronic materials, structures, and processes available to us for the innovation of integrated electronics. We will not list them here; there are too many and they are too specialized for general discussion. Just felt me say that we are blessed, or caused, with a technological feast that can jade our judgment.

When innovators are choosing from such a long menu, each must have a clear idea of his long-term objectives. What are we innovating *for*? What kinds of systems are we developing for what markets? What business do we want to be in? Only when he answers these questions can he develop his unique long-term strategies. In electronics today, each innovator will have his own unique set of cost-effectiveness measures determined by his choice of markets. But besides these approximately different classical measures, each innovator must now include in his strategy the new measure of *adaptability* of a technology.

By way of example, but only that, let me show how the overall *objective* of the Bell System—and an *adaptive* strategy—have guided our choices of materials and process for our innovation of integrated electronics.

Let me restate the Bell System's simple goal: "To provide the best communications service to the lowest cost consistent with financial health." As we said in order *always* to meet this goal, we must seek continuing innovation. But the systems nature of our business demands that all the parts, old and new, of our large network must work compatibility and continually. Both for continuous service and financial health, our complex network cannot be scrapped and rebuilt in whole, or in large part, every few years. It must operate satisfactorily while it is being maintained and transformed. At the risk of sounding overdramatic: "Innovation in such a system is like getting a heart transplant while running a four-minute mile!"

Nationwide communications also require a wide variety of electrical functions. We need all the digital functions of logic, memory, switching, and pulse transmission. The speeds we deal with range from a few pulses per second to greater than 500 million per second. Memory requirements cover the full gamut: access times from thousandths to billionths of a second, and capacities from thousands to hundreds of million of information bits. In the analogue field, we need all known functions: modulators, demodulators, filters, oscillators, amplifiers, and access transducers—over the full frequency spectrum. Amplifier bandwidth is never great enough; noise and distortion are never low enough. The only performance dimension we do not cover is that of power, though we need ranges from millionths of a watt to watts. In short, our requirements for performance cover most of those for all other markets.

Finally, the marketing service, rather than product, requires a different balance between performance, cost, and reliability; and it differs for each of the different functions and environments met in transmission, switching, and customer systems. Service is measured by the kind and amount of performance per annual dollar of expense. Annual expense includes manufacturing cost, installation cost, and maintenance expense of systems, in addition to the amortized cost of land and buildings. As systems increase in complexity and as labor costs rise, assembly, wiring, installation, and maintenance become increasing fractions of our annual expense. Reliability and batch fabrication to the highest systems level become essential criteria for our innovations. But the size and diversity of our system, the need for compatibility of *all* its parts, and the demand for continuity of its service make for long and costly innovation. All these properties requires that our network *and its technology* be highly adaptive. For these reasons, we have chosen a more complex hybrid approach to integration; it contains not one material-system but several, depending upon the state of the art and the systems functions required. We have chosen this approach because we believe it has higher adaptability than the monolithic planar silicon system, and we have designed it for total batch fabrication.

Currently, the hybrid system is composed of two different but complementary material-systems, each of which can have many variations. One is based on the electronic functions available with diffused silicon; the other depends upon the electronic functions of thin metal films on ceramic substrates.

As in planar silicon technology, our so-called "beam-lead sealed junction" technology uses oxide masking, photolithography, and diffusion to define the structure of the silicon circuit elements. But it uses a more complex metal-insulator system, along with the silicon, to provide batch fabrication of the complete subsystem. No costly one-at-a-time finishing operations are required. Figure shows a pair of complementary but compatible silicon subsystems. At the left is a memory subsystem; it will store 128 bits of information and requires 768 interconnected elements to do this. On the right is the associated switch to afford access to the memory chip. It contains 344 diodes, transistors, and resistors. Since the functions of each we significantly different, for optimum performance, cost, and reliability of each, we use different metal-insulator—silicon subsystems. As can be seen their termination leads have been batch-fabricated all at one time. What is not apparent is that no costly one-at-a-time protective enclosures are required. Our particular materials system provides in situ protection of all elements—and it is provided as part of the batchfabrication process. Thus, the one-at-a-time termination-capsulation operations are eliminated. Equally important, as will be seen, these chips are compatible for batch interconnection.

To provide such interconnection—and the highly precise, stable resistors can capacitors which silicon cannot provide—we use thin-metal-film technology. This subsystem starts with thin films of tantalum of controlled chemical and physical structure. By altering film composition and structure, we can design for a wide range of electric properties. Using the same photolithography process as for silicon, we can define the topology of resistors and capacitors and their circuit intraconnections.

Using batch oxidation of the tantalum, we can trim resistors and capacitors to high precision; and the oxidation provides contaminant protection for the resistive films and insulators for capacitors simulataneouly. Thus, as in our silicon system, terminations and capsulation are provided as part of the batch process—there are no one-at-a-time operations in this subsystem either. Finally, to provide hybrid systems, we batch-film subsystems.

The adaptability of our hybrid technology to some of the functions needed for the Bell System. In each case, the partitioning between silicon chips, and between silicon and thin-film subsystems, is determined by the functional requirements and the current economics of the two materials technologies. For example, the 1,024-bit memory module contains 32 silicon chips of 32 memory bits each and 12 silicon access circuits. As our yields improve, we can increase the number of bits per silicon chip—or we can even shift easily to a different memory subsystem, if desired.

Next, to the right, is a hybrid system for Touch-tone dialing in the telephone set, and on the extreme right is a microwave-amplifier module needed for long-haul transmission systems. As our technology improves, we expect to integrate several modules as a single system.

To sum up, both material subsystems use batch fabrication for all process steps up to their interface. Since they also match at their interface in topology and metallurgy, they are compatible as well as complementary in function—they can be batch-interconnected to form hybrid systems for the high reliability and wide range of analogue and digital performance our systems require. Since they are independently batch-fabricated and tested, hybrid yields are the average, not the product, of subsystem yields.

Thus, the choice of how much function is assigned to each silicon and thin-film subsystem is flexible. Tradeoffs between cost and performance can be made easily. The interface between the two materials can shift flexibly for different systems, and with the improvements that are coming in each materials technology. For new electronic functions, such as those available from laser and electroluminescence phenomena, new materials are required. By extending beam-lead sealed-junction principles to these different semiconductors, they become synergistic parts of our present technology.

We believe this approach to integration can provide "RSI," the *right scale of integration*, for each of our many different systems. We believe that RSI is, above all, an *adaptive* technology, that it can survive and be renewed for many years to come, as our present technologies improve, as our systems need change, and as new materials functions are added.

When you are in the "innovation business," it is easy to get caught up in past successes to the extent that you forget why you are innovating in the first place. You keep doing more of the same thing, only bigger and better—not necessarily because you know it is right, but because it seems natural and *easy* to do more of the same. Perhaps this is why some artists keep painting the same picture, or why some writers keep telling the same story in book after book—or why SSTs seem logical to some people. In technological innovation, this can be a deadly trap—it takes you eye off changing goals and criteria. You forget to seek new viewpoints, to look for new potential solutions. Or, very importantly, you forget to seek new criteria, like adaptability, for making choices. Let me give you another example.

Our present hybrid tcchnology is indeed powerful and adaptive. It does use batch fabrication throughout and is flexible enough to meet our wide variety of markets. But it achieves its power and adaptability by requiring a large number of serial process steps—to change the microscopic structure of silicon and metal films so that indeed these few materials can perform many different functions within themselves. But, what if we could find a mateial-system which required *fewer* batch process steps? What if indeed the physical phenomena *themselves*were generically more adaptive? Then we might have a simpler system. This indeed is a tall order. The physical phenomena of semiconductors are highly versatile—today's integrated electronics proves that—and we still have a lot of potential to tap. But let us look only at digital information processing for the moment. Functions such as logic, memory, and switching are needed, and we have to use many process steps in semiconductors to perform all these different functions in a single piece of silicon. Is it possible to find a single material for our purpose, and a set of physical phenomena which do not require so many microscopic structure changes to adapt the single material to the different functions required? Is there indeed a material phenomenon which is more adaptive than the transistor effect for digital functions? We have asked such heretical questions and it appears that the answer *may* be yes. As a result, in Bell Laboratories, device physicists and materials researchers are hard at work on a new technology that is based on the controlled nucleation, transport, and detection of tiny "magnetic bubbles," or domains, in ferromagnetic materials. If this technology proves to be as powerful and adaptive as we hope, then one day it will be possible to perform such functions as logic, memory, switching and display withina single piece of *homogeneous* material—at great savings in cost, power, and size. Indeed, since we could then economically mix logic and memory on a microscopic basis within the homogeneous material, we might be able to change the basic architecture of data-processing machines to make them more adaptive and less costly and cumbersome to build and program. We cite this example not because we sure it will happen. Rather, we sure only that we would not be doing this work if some Demon had not taken a new viewpoint and asked a new question—at the very time when semiconductor technology was riding high.

And this is precisely how the ecological view of organisations prompts the manager. It leads him to ask new questions about the innovative organisation and to pose new criteria that a technology should meet for effective innovation. Once again: Ask an important question—you just might get an important answer. Beyond knowing the cost-effectiveness requirements of his particular markets, the ecologically oriented manager applies the additional yardstick of adaptability to his choice of technology. Only by doing so can he have any assurance that the long and total process of innovation will bring him an adequate return. Only if his choice is truly an adaptive one will he be sure that the selected technology will survive long enough to meet his present and future markets. For remember, the technological environment is changing all the time.

Thus, to meet the criterion of adaptability for his choice of technology, the manager must have a clear idea of his present and future markets, their cost-effectiveness requirements, and how they will change. He must see how his chosen technology, and its competing technologies, may be affected by the evolution of new knowledge, new physical phenomena, and new material-systems. The technology he chooses must be able to adapt to all these changes. It must be able to absorb and use them—to get an investment payoff—before becoming obsolete.

3 Control in Organisation

Man's life in contemporary society can be characterized largely as one of organisational memberships. Man commits a major portion of his waking hours to participation in at least one, and more often several, social organisations. His motivation, his aspirations, his general way of life, are tied inextricably to the organisations of which he is a part, and even to some of which he is not.

Organisations are of vital interest to the social scientist, because one finds within them an important juncture between the individual and the collectivity. Out of this juncture comes much in our pattern of living that has been the subject of both eulogy and derogation. That man derives a great deal from organisational membership leaves little to be argued; that he often pays heavily for the benefits of organisational membership seems an argument equally compelling. At the heart of this exchange lies the process of control.

Characterizing an organisation in terms of its pattern of control is to describe an essential and universal aspect of organisation which every member must face and to which he must adjust.

Organisation implies control. A social organisation is an ordered arrangement of individual human interactions. Control processes help circumscribe idiosyncratic bahaviours and keep them conformant to the rational plan of the organisation. Organisations require a certain amount of conformity as well as the integration of diverse activities. It is the function of control to bring about conformance to organisational requirements and achievement of the ultimate purposes of the organisation. The coordination and order created out of the diverse interests and potentially diffuse behaviours of members is largely a function of control. It is at this point that many of the problems of organisational functioning and of individual adjustment arise.

Control is an inevitable correlate of organisation. But it is more than this. It is concerned with aspects of social life that are of the utmost importance to everyone. It is concerned with questions of the common will and the common weal.

The problems control and conformity in organisations contribute to a serious dilemma. Organisation provides order-a condition necessary for man to produce abundantly and live securely. there certainly are differences of opinion regarding the definition of these conditions that form the basis for human freedom. Yet social order itself requires conformity and imposes limitations. Furthermore, the responsibility for creating and sustaining order tends to be distributed unevenly within organisations. Often it is the few who decide on the kind of order to which the many must conform. But regardless of how orders is created, it requires the conformity of all or nearly all to organisational norms.

Some conceptions of control

Control has been variously defined, and different terms are sometimes used synonymously with it. Its original application in business organisations derives from the French usage meaning to check. It is now commonly used in a broader sense synonymously with the notions of influence and power. We shall use the term in this way to refer to any process in which a person or group of persons or organisation of persons/determines, that is, internationally affects, the behaviour of another person, group, or organisation.

Although our definition conforms essentially to what many authors mean by control, power, or influence, there certainly are differences of opinion regarding the definition of these terms. For example, some writers prefer to think of power as an exclusively coercive form of control. Weber was the first of the classic authors on organisation to reject this limited notion of power, and many contemporary social scientists, including the authors of this volume, are inclined to think of power as having bases in addition to, although by no means excluding, coercive ones. Some authors like to think of power in terms of differentials or ratios that describe the relative "strength" of persons in a system. In this view power is essentially the effect that one person has on a second compared with that which the second has on the first. This is an important index of power relations, but we see it conceptually as a derivative of the more general definition that we propose. A number of authors prefer to distinguish power from control by defining power essentially as the ability or capacity to exercise control, that is as "potential control." Compare, for example, Goldhamer and Shils's definition with that of Etzioni. According to the former, "a person may be said to have power to the extent that he influences the behaviour of others in accordance with his own intentions"; according to the second, "power is an actor's ability to induce or influence another actor to carry out his directives or any other norms he supports". Both these definitions are consistent in essential respects with our own, although Etzioni's statement implies what we should prefer to call potential control. For most authors the term *authority* usually refers to the formal right to exercise control, and we follow this general convention in the article that follow.

The meaning of control, as we define it, can be seen in the simple prototype in Figure, which represents control as a cycle beginning with an intent on the part of the person, followed by an influence attempt addressed to another person, who then acts in some way that fulfills the intent of the first. There are, of course, many elements in addition to those indicated that are important in understanding this process. These include the assumptions and values of the actors, the "bases of power" that help explain B's response, and the great variety of means by which A attempts to influence B. Such means may be direct or indirect; they may include orders or requests, threats or promises, and so fourth. The behaviour of B may involve relationships with other persons or it may involve actions in relation to technological elements, such as tools, computers, or production lines. Thus technology may enter in to the cycle at various points, creating what has been called a "sociotechnical" system. For example, computers may provide A with information that leads him to request B to do one thing rather than another. Or A simply use the computer to tell B. A may also speed up a production line, which illustrates another form of influence attempt on B.

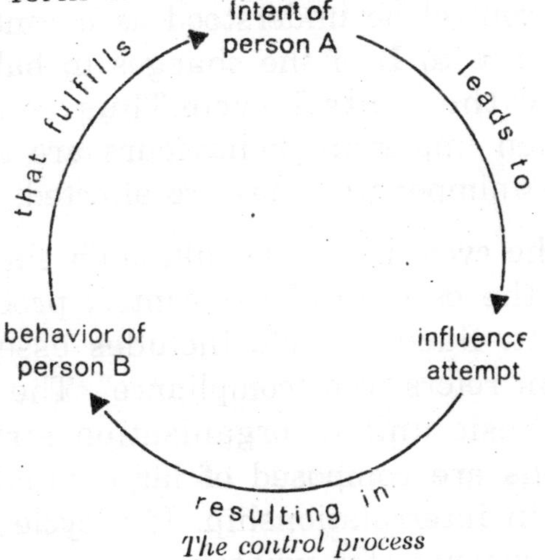

The control process

The intentions of A may be initiated by him, or they may be the intentions of others that are acquired by A. These intentions may imply quite specific actions for B, as when a supervisor gives detailed instructions to a subordinate; or they may be very general, although no less real, as in the formulation of organisational policy. The hebaviour of B, which is the object of A's intentions, may in our definition, be covert as well as overt. A, for example, may have intentions regarding the intentions of B, and vice versa.

When we say that A determines B's bahaviour, we mean that A "causes" B to behave in an intended way. Control, the, is a special case of social causation Dahl has provided a useful conceptualization of this point by defining the control of A over B as the probability it in the absence of the request. In an elaboration of Dahl's definition, Tennenbaum has proposed that the amount of control be understood as a function of the importance to B of the changes in bahaviour affected by the control cycle.Thus control is greater when important behaviours are affected than when unimportant ones are affected.

Thus the cycle in Figure, although simplified, represents the essence of the control process, as we define it. Such a cycle includes essentially what Etzioni refers to a "compliance". The control cycle is a basic unit of organisation structure; organisations are composed of large numbers of such cycle in interrelationship. If a cycle breaks down at any point, for whatever reason, control cannot be said to exist. For example, A may have conflicting intents that lead to confusing influence attempts and hence to a breakdown in the cycle; or B may be incapable of fulfilling A's request, even though B may which to or B may dislike A and so refuse to do A's bidding; or B may be included in two or more cycles that involve contradictory influence attempts; and so on. Chronic breakdowns of such cycles imply a breakdown in the organisation itself.

Traditional analyses of control

Although the theoretical analysis of control in social systems has a long and venerable history, empirical research on this subject has been initiated only recently in organisations. The "human-relations" approach that inspired a great deal of research in organisation avoided explicit reference to social power or control, partly because these terms carried connotations that were inconsistent with the ideal of the harmonious, conflict-free organisation. Traditionally, the concept of power has been associated with forms of tyranny, elitism or authoriutarism, or with conflict and struggle. Almost all the literature on the power of leadership, according to Bell, stems from the works of Aristotle and Machiavelli and is committed to "the image of the mindless masses and the image of the strong-willed leader." Historically, ideologies of management have grown up, according to Bendix, specifically to justify the employers' exercise of authority, which was associated in one way or another with the subordination or exploitation of workers.

According to Michels's classic conception, control in organisations must inevitably become oligarchic. Michels's "iron law of oligarchy" applies even to political organisations that begin democratically and are committed to a democratic ideology. Leaders themselves are incapable of deflecting this historic process; democratic and idealistic leaders succumb eventually to the corruption inherent in power. Michels cites a number of arguments in support of the tendency toward oligarchy in organisations. First, the rank and file, through incompetence and apathy, cannot and do not which to exercise control, the masses prefer to be led. Second, democracy is structurally impossible in large and complex social system; there is no way of arranging the system so that the views of the many individual members can be heard and taken into account. The impracticality of democracy is especially apparent in organisations undergoing conflict with others. Especially during periods of crisis, organisations need form leadership and precise adherence to orders. Finally, the tendency toward oligarchy results from the character of leaders and the role that they must play. Because of their cultural and educational superiority over the masses, leaders form a distinct elite. The status, perquisites, and privileges associated with the leadership role serve further to separate the leaders from the masses. In labor unions and socialist parties, for example, the life of the leaders becomes that of the petite bourgeoisie. Leaders therefore develop a vested interest in their position, which they must product. Furthermore, a personal lust for power, which is characteristic of leaders, intensifies their efforts to enhance their power, and leaders resort to ulterior devices towards this end. In "democratic" parties leaders employ emotional and demagogic appeals to manipulate the gullible masses. They control the party press, using it to describe themselves in the most favourable light, while deriding their opposition within the party. They exploit their special information and knowledge of the organisation too outmaneuver opponents. And, if despite these tactics, the leaders are overthrown, the new office holders, in turn, undergo the inevitable "transformation which renders them in every respect similar to the dethroned tyrants.... The revolutionaries of today become the reactionaries of tomorrow".

Some changes in the conception of control

Michels's pessimism about democracy in organisations in reflected, in one form or another in the work of a number of contemporary organisation theorists. Goulder has wondered why these theorists focus so tenaciously on the constraints inherent in organisation that thwart democracy, while failing to consider the constrains that may contribute to the realization of democratic aspirations. Why is it that 'unanticipated consequences' are always tacitly assumed to be destructive to democratic values and 'bad'; why can't they sometimes he 'good?' Are there no constraints which *force* men to adhere valorously to their democratic beliefs, which *compel* them to be intelligent rather than blind, which leave them *no choice* but to be men of good will rather than predators?"

Many of the classical conceptions of control, including those of Webber in bureaucracies and Muchels in political organisations, have proved valuable in analyses of contemporary organisations, the changing character of societies and organisations over the years is making apparent some of the limitations of those older conceptions. The emphasis in contemporary social science on quantitative research has also contributed to changes in interpretations of he control process because of the need to develop conceptions that are operations as well as theoretically meaningful. At the same time, research findings themselves have led to reinterpretations of older conceptions.

The increasing numbers and complexity of organisations in modern industrial societies require large numbers or persons with a high level of technical and administrative expertise to play leadership roles. The demand for expert leaders reduces the suitability of those recruited on the basis of social status or family connections. Achievement replaces ascription as the basis for placing leaders, and their recruitment spreads to all strata of society. Similarly, political criteria, prevalent as the basis of recruitment during early stages in newly independent and in revolutionary societies, become less important. At the same time, training centers for leaders are established in universities, business schools, and training institutes, and the possibility for careers in industrial leadership is opened to large or persons. Management becomes professionalized. Although these developments are most apparent in business and industrial organisations and in some agencies of government, they are also occurring in other organisations, including the military and labor unions.

Most of these changes imply a rationalization of the control process in organisations consistent with Weber's bureaucratic model. However, further changes in the way leaders exercise control are likely to accompany this rationalization, and these represent a divergence from the classical bureaucratic model. Leaders may rely on discussion and persuasion rather than on command exclusively. Attempts may be made to elicit cooperation, sometimes by having organisation members participate in the making of decisions that affect them in the work place. The rising level of education of the work force represents an important "constraint" that contributes to this trend. In addition the specialized skills that are frequently required of persons at all levels in modern organisations may sometimes mean that subordinates are more expert in a particular specialization than their superiors, thus modifying the classical supervisory-subordinate relationship. Furthermore, professional managers are more inclined than their predecessors to consider the results of social research, such as that described in this book, which have supported the growth of human-relations approaches to control in organisations. At the same time, political developments, particularly in some European countries, have led to the introduction of schemes of comanagement and of workers' councils, with varying degrees of success. These developments may not be fully consolidated in any contemporary society, but incipient support, at least can be found in many organisations for less autocratic control than was customary in the past. A survey in fourteen industrialized and developing nations, for example, shows that managers overwhelmingly subscribe at least to the idea of participation by workers in decision making, although managers express skepticism about the capacity of workers to assume the responsibilities consonant with democratic leadership.

Taken together, these developments imply the growth—actual in some places, potential in others—of new kinds of control in addition to those prevalent in the past. Partly as a consequence of this end of developments in research, conceptions of the control process have been broadened.

First, a change has taken place in analyses of the bases of power. Coercion has played a prominent role in traditional analyses, consistent with the presumed conflict between leaders and followers. Leaders are obeyed out of fear of punishment or hope for reward. Weber, however, argues that the stability of social systems depends on acceptance by followers of the right of leaders to exercise control. This implies legitimate authority, and Weber defines three types: (1) "Charismatic" authority, according to which leaders are thought to be endowed with extraordinary, sometimes magical powers. Charisma on the part of a leader elicits obedience out of awe. It is illustrated in its pure form by "the prophet, the warrior hero, the great demagogue". (2) "Traditional" authority, which appertains to those who have the right to rule by virtue of birth or class. The traditional leader is obeyed because he or members of his class or family has always been followed. It pure type is illustrated by certain patriarchs, monarchs, and feudal lords. (3) "Legal" authority, which applies to those who hold leadership positions because of demonstrated technical competence. Legal authorities act impersonally as instruments of the law, and they are obeyed impersonally our of a sense of duty to the law. Leadership in the ideal bureaucracy is based exclusively on legal authority.

The character of authority envisioned within this framework is consistent with many of the traditional analyses: Weber's authority figures are prophets, warriors, demagogues, patriarchs, lords, and bureaucrats. More recent analyses have stressed bases of power in addition to those outlined by Weber.

Simon, for example, points to the importance of social approval. Approval and disapproval represent forms of reward and punishment, but they deserve special consideration because they are frequently dispensed, not only by the designed leader, but also by others. Thus, a subordinate may obey a supervisor, not so much because of the rewards and punishments meted out by the supervisor, as because of the approval and disapproval by the subordinate's own peers. Confidence may represent a further basis for acceptance of leaders' authority. A subordinate may trust the judgment and therefore accept the authority of a leader in areas where the leader has great technical competence. Frech and Raven make a further distinction between the influence of a leader based on confidence by subordinates in the leaders' expert knowledge and "informational influence" based on acceptance by subordinates of the logic of the arguments that the leader offers. An expert leader, then, may exercise control, not simply because he is an acknowledged authority, but because his decisions, being based on expertise, are manifestly logical, appropriate, and convincing. Subordinates are persuaded that the decisions are correct. This is related to some human-relations approaches that stress control by facts as opposed to control by men. Such "fact control" relies on understanding, and is illustrated by the participative leader who influences the behaviour of subordinates by helping them understand the facts of a situation so that they may jointly arrive at a course of action consistent with their own interests and that of the collectivity. Some of these conceptions represent radical departures from many traditional ones, assuming, as they do, an overriding community of interests among all members of the organisation.

A further change in the conception of power relates to assumptions concerning the mutuality-unilaterality of control. A view common to traditional analyses argues that the control process is unilateral; one either leads or is led, is strong or weak, controls or is controlled. Simmel, in spite of his general adherence to the traditional conflict view of power, noted a more subtle intersection underlying the appearance of "pure superiority" on the part of one person and the "purely passive being led" of another. "All leaders are also led; in innumerable cases the master is the slave of his slaves". Contemporary analyses are more likely than earlier ones to consider relationships of mutual as well as unilateral power, of followers influencing leaders, as well as vice versa.

Finally, traditional analyses of social power assume that the total amount of power in a social system is a fixed quantity and that leaders and followers are engaged in a "zero sum game": increasing the power of the one party must be accompanied by a corresponding decrease in the power of the other. Some social scientists are now inclined to question the generality of this assumption. The total amount of power in a social system may grow, and leaders and followers may therefore enhance their power jointly. Total power may also decline, and all groups within the system may suffer corresponding decreases.

The total amount of control in an organisation

The issue of total amount of control in a system has been of concern to social scientists more implicitly than explicitly. Most analyses of control have been concerned with the relative control exercised by groups within organisations rather than with the total amount. The literature, therefore, provides little guidance concerning the conditions under which the amount of control in a system may expand.

In principle this expansion may occur under either of two classes of conditions. The first is that of an external expansion of power into the organisation's environment. The second concerns a number of internal conditions that subsume (1) structural conditions expediting interaction and influence among members and (2) motivational conditions implying increased interest by members in exercising control and a greater amenability by members to being controlled. These conditions may sometimes be related. For example, extending control by the organisation into its environment may bring more decisions within the purview of the organisation that are subject to the control of its members, thus increasing the possibility of a greater total amount of control. At the same time such increased opportunities to exercise control within the organisation may increase the members' involvement in and identification with the organisation and hence increase their interest in exercising control and their amenability to being controlled. Members, then as possible control agents, engage in more frequent influence attempts, and as possible objects of control, provide new opportunities to one another to exercise control. Thus external developments may affect special and psychological processes within the organisation conducive to a high level of internal control, just as conditions of a high level of involvement by members and of a high level of control within the organisation may contribute to the strength of the organisation and hence to its power in its environments. Several general concepts in current use are helpful in describing how the above conditions may contribute to the expansion of control within a social system.

Control and exchange

The first concept is that of "exchange of resources," as discussed by Blau, Deutsch, Homan, Lasswell and Kaplan, and Thibaut and Kelley. For example, Homan suggests that a "sense of justice" demands that a person who has received much from another should also give much to him. The exercise of control may be viewed as an exchange of some valued resource dispensed by one person in return for compliance on the part of the another. The total amount of control or power in a system may therefore be seen as a function of the amount of exchange involving compliance. This amount may change, because the quantity of resources among members changes or because of a change in the rules regarding exchange. For example, in increase in affectional ties among members may lead to the growth of social approval as a resource, because approval is valued more from liked persons than from those not liked. Hence social systems composed of persons who like one another can, in principle, engage in a greater amount of exchange of approval for compliance than systems composed of persons who are indifferent to one another. In simplest terms. A does what B requests, because A values B's approval, and B does what A requests, because he values A's approval. Or A does what B requests, because he values B's approval, and B does what A requests because "justice demands" that B reciprocate.

Traditional managerial approaches can be distinguished from participative by the rules regarding the quality and quantity of exchange within them. In some traditional systems employees exchange compliance for pay; in participative systems they do so for some managerial compliance, thus increasing the total amount of compliance. The possibility of such an expanding exchange relies heavily on the assumption of broad areas of common interest (rather than conflict) between members and leaders of the organisation.

Control and partial inclusion

A second concept that may be helpful in describing how control expands within a system is that of "partial inclusion," suggested by Allport. Organisational behaviour involves only a limited segment of the many needs and the potential repertory of behaviour that define the total make-up of members as individuals. In their role as organisation members individuals do not express the full range of their personalities; they are thus only "partially included" in the organisation. Because only a part of the members is included, only a part of him is at the disposal, so to speak, of the organisation. Thus there are limitations to the range of activities that are subject to influence; excluded from influence is that large segment of the person that does not belong to the organisation. Bureaucracy was designed precisely to exclude this segment, not as a means of restricting members, but as a mans of protecting them from undue and illegitimate control.

Including members more fully in the organisation can be viewed can be viewed as an expansion of the organisation into its environment, because the newly included segments of the individual were heretofore outside the organisation. More things to be controlled now fall within the purview of the organisation, and hence there is opportunity for some members at least to increase their control without necessarily reducing that exercised by others.

Anything that enhances members' personal commitment to or identification with the organisation is implicitly including them more fully within the organisation and hence is increasing the possibility of an expanded total amount of control. Human-relations approaches that are designed to increase the identification of members may therefore result in greater inclusion and greater control. Similarly, giving members some influence in the organisation generally has the effect of increasing their identification with the organisation and their inclusion it. Hence increasing members' influence may also increase their influenceability, and so contributing to a higher level of control in the system.

Control and negative entropy

A third concept that may help describe the meaning of the total amount of control in an organisation is that of "negative entropy," which is an index of order. Order is the essence of organisation; organisational behaviour is ordered behaviour. This order applies to what goes on within the organisation at a particular moment as well as to the regularity of the organisation through time. However, the natural tendency of all systems is toward disorder, or entropy. "This tending toward entropy is, so far as we know, a universal law of nature". Hence in social organisations, as in all systems that are to maintain their orderliness, there is a need for some means of negating the entropic tendency. Control is part of the means for meeting this essential requirement. For this reason organisation is inconceivable without some system of control.

The function of control in reducing the amount of entropy in organisations can be seen through a comparison of the actions of persons who are behaving on the basis of their purely individualistic inclinations without regard for organisational requirements and persons who are behaving in organisational roles. The former tend, as a group, to show in their behaviour a considerable degree of randomness. For example, persons arise at widely disparate hours and come and go according to their many diverse, personal, and idiosyncratic interests. Their behaviour along given dimensions thus tends to be distributed according to the normal probability curve, following the usual distribution of personality traits. This randomness, in the "collective" behaviour of persons displays a high degree of entropy. As organisation members, however, their collective behavior is more controlled and less entropic. One, although not the only, manifestation of this reduced entropy can be found in the uniformities that characterize some of the bahaviour of organisation members. Allport provides a graphic illustration, through the hypothetical curves in Figure 3, of the uniformity and orderliness of behaviour implied by organisation. "The narrow, more uniform distribution demonstrates the effects of social control, adherence or conformity by members to some organisational rule or standard. It also illustrates one aspect of the order and predictability essential to organisation; we know or can predict within a relatively narrow margin of error, where a particular person is likely to fall on the scale if he is a member of a group whose behaviour distribute according to the solid-line curve. Most persons in this group fall within a very narrow range. In the case of the dashed-line curve, however, our prediction would be less certain and less reliable—as would an organisation built on distribution of this kind".

The second law of thermodynamics states that a system tends toward its most probable state, which, for the hypothetical groups portrayed in the above curves, is the normal probability distribution—unless a reduction of entropy is achieved and maintained to forestall the inevitable deterioration into randomness. Since control is a means of creating order organisations that doffer in their orderliness may be expected to differ in the amounts of control within them. The limiting case f the laissez-faire, anarchic organisation, characterized by a high degree of entropy, is relatively little controlled. The move away from *laissez faire*, whether toward a more democratic, autocratic, or polyarchic system of control, is a move toward more orderliness and more control. This is consistent with the argument that organisations should be viewed, not simply as all-or-none phenomena, but as variable states. The total amount of control, like negative entropy, may be taken as one index of degree of organisation.

Control and graph theory

The notions of graph theory may also be helpful in conceptualizing the total amount of control as a variable in a group or organisation. Graph theory calls attention to the "connections" between points in a network. A limiting case is a set of points that are not connected at all. This may represent a social "network" in which the individuals are isolated socially from one another; hence there is no control within this system. Figure 4, taken from Frech, illustrates hypothetical networks that differ in their connectedness and total amounts of control. Set A, a "weakly connected" set, manifests little change through time in the attitudes of members. Set B, a "completely connected" set, shows a great deal of change toward a single, uniform attitude position. This set has a high total amount of control within it—and less entropy.

Graph theory is helpful in describing many kinds of social relations. For example, an acquaintanceship between two persons is weakly connected; hence it manifests little internal control in comparison with an intimate friendship, which is strongly connected and hence high in control. Some relationships may vary through time in their connectedness. For example, an acquaintanceship may evolve into a more intimate relationship. Or particular classes of relationships, such as families, may include cases that differ in their connectedness and the amounts of control within them. For example, some families are more tightly knit than others. In the former, members engage in more activities together, and they interact and influence on another more substantially. There is more to the family in this case and hence more to be controlled. Similarly, the cohesive group is characterized by more connectedness and hence more control than the noncohesive group. Furthermore such groups may themselves be conceived graph-theoretically as points that can be connected. An organisation represented by strong connections between such points each of which itself represents a set of strongly connected points, is an organisation high in total amount of control in comparison with one that is weakly connected.

Some approaches to enhancing the total amount of control

Several authors illustrate, through a number of relatively specific "mechanisms," the possibility of increasing the total amount of control in organisations. For example, Selznick's cooptation principle implies, at least under some circumstances, a degree of influence exercised within the organisation by the coopted element, which it did not exercise before cooptation, as well as an increased control by the "hierarchy" over the coopted element. Aspects of "participative management" share some features with cooptation. For example, the more complete inclusion through participation of "partially included" members may be viewed as a form of cooptation. Similarly, through participation, cohesive informal groups may be coopted by the formal organisation.

Some of the control-enhancing features of the participative approach can be seen with respect to the supervisor-subordinate relationship. One can easily picture the laissez-faire leader who exercises little control over his subordinates and who at the same time may be indifferent to their wishes. He neither influences nor is influenced by his men. A second, more participative supervisor interacts and communicates often, welcomes opinions, and elicits influence attempts. Suggestions that subordinates offer make a difference to him, and his subordinates are responsive, in turn, to his requests. To the extent that the organisational hierarchy from top to bottom is characterized in this way, we have a highly integrated, tightly knit social system. We have, in the terms of Likert, a more substantial interaction influence system—and a greater total amount of control.

Participative systems of management that conform to what Miles calls the "human-resources" model imply a more active involvement of members in the organisation and a higher total amount of control than is typical of most bureaucracies. The human-resources model, which Miles sees emerging in the writings of McGregor, Likert, Haire, and others, assumes that members have capabilities (resource) that are not ordinarily exploited in the organisation. Some of these capabilities can be used by the organisation, just as the organisation can be used by these capabilities, in the sense that the organisation is a means through which the capabilities can be realized. Hence there is a greater identification, objectively as well as subjectively, between the member and the collectivity; the action that represent fulfilment of the heretofore excluded capabilities of members are, in the human-resources model, an integral part of the organisation. Furthermore, these capabilities, and the needs associated with them, are active and, in some degree, directing elements in the system; they help define "intents" in the cycles of actions and interactions of members that *are* the organisation.

"Mechanistic" and "organic" models of organisation, described by Bruns and Stalker and by Shepard and Blake, imply differences in the total amount of control. The mechanistic organisation characterized by a hierarchic structure of control and "precise definition of rights and obligations" of members, as in the traditional bureaucracy. The organic system, which is more like the human resources model has a network structure of control. The effectiveness on control in this type of organisation derives more from the member's deep involvement and "presumed community of interest with the rest of the working organisation in the survival and growth of the firm,... from a contractual relationship between himself and a non-personal cooperation...". The network system of control and the involvement of members in their organisational roles implies a highly integrated system. As a consequence the organic organisation is more flexible, or adaptable, than the mechanistic. For example, the mechanistic organisation may adapt to an environmental change by creating a special group within the organisation to protect it from change. This group may be relatively isolated from the rest of the organisation. In the organic organisation, on the other hand, members respond and adjust mutually and integratively to change. The reaction here is holistic; adaptation is a "concerted response of the firm" in which all members play a part. The highly coordinated response of the organic system implies a relatively high level of control by as well as over all organisation members. The total amount of control in the organic system is therefore relatively high compared with the mechanistic.

Organisations constructed on the basis of overlapping "organisation families," as proposed by Likert and Mann conform, in a number of respects, to the organic model. To achieve this type of organisation, Likert proposes that each supervisor must form his subordinates into a highly cohesive work, group, called an organisational family in which he is a member. Supervisors, in turn, are members of a second set of highly cohesive groups with their superiors, who are members of a third set, and so on, up the organisational hierarchy. Most supervisors, therefore are members of two groups, one in which they act as supervisors with their subordinates and one in which they are subordinates along with their own peers. Thus the effects of the high level of control generated within the tightly knit organisational families are coordinated by the supervisors, who act as "linking pins" between groups.

An analysis by Likert of some departments that conform to this model led to the conclusion that the "managers have actually increased the size of the `influence pie' by means of the leadership processes which they use. They listen more to their men, are more interested in their men's ideas, and have more confidence and trust in their men." There is a greater give-and-take and supportiveness by superiors and a higher level of effective communications upward, downward, and sideward. This all contributes to a greater sensitivity and receptivity on the part of each organisation member to the influence of others—superiors relative to subordinates and subordinates relative to superiors. There is in these departments a higher level of mutual control and a more likely integration of the interests of workers, supervisors, and managers.

The participative system distinguishes itself from the traditional bureaucracy by the extent to which members are personally involved. The deeper, personal commitment of members is one of the bases for the success of the participative approach, but it is also the basis for interpersonal complications and possible conflicts that are precisely what Weber hoped, through bureaucracy, to avoid. Participative models, therefore, require interpersonal skills and sophistication of members, as well as acceptance of values and assumptions that are not called for in more traditional models. Training laboratory techniques, including sensitivity training, the T group, and the managerial grid, represent approaches to meeting this requirement. Such training, when associated with appropriate structural changes and delegations of authority in an organisation, may contribute to the total enhancement of control through contributing to competencies that permit persons to interrelate more "sensitively" and thus to resolve conflicts and reduce resistances that otherwise would stand in the way of effective interaction and influence. If it is effective, laboratory training may also foster confidence and trust that lead to acceptance by each member of the intents, rather than simply the orders, of others. Sensitivity to and acceptance of intents reduces "noise," for example, misunderstandings or defensive reactions, that otherwise might enter into the impede the control cycles.

The relatively high level of control in many participative models does not fit common stereotypes that assume participation to be a vaguely permissive or laissez-faire system—or some kind of dictatorship of the proletariat. Participative models that conform to such stereotypes justify the arguments of opponents who maintain that participation is not feasible in a work organisation. There is no escaping the need for some system of control in organisations, including participations. These organisations are not practical unless they have an effective system of control through which the potentially diverse interests and action of members are integrated into concerted, that is, organized, bahaviour. The relative success of participative approaches, therefore, hinges, not on reducing control, but on achieving a system of control that is more effective than that of other systems. In some organisations there may be a lot of order giving but relatively little control because of structural and motivational breakdowns in the control cycles. The participative model is designed to overcome these obstacles. Thus, there may be relatively little order giving, as such, in participative system, but the influence attempts that are made are effective; that is, they eventuate in control.

The high level of control implicit in organic, participative models can be understood in terms of the general concepts previously described. Participative models imply strong connectedness through structural arrangements. Such as overlapping organisational families; high total, as opposed to partial, inclusion of members by utilizing more of their capacities and fostering their identification with the organisation; a large stock of resources, such as social approval or skills of various kinds, that are exchanged for compliance; and low entropy through reduction of misunderstandings, conflicts, and resistances.

The measurement of control in organisations

A serious problem in studies of control is that of measurement. In general, researchers have obtained data bout control either from available records describing the legal or structural characteristics of organisations or from informants who respond to questions concerning how or where in the organisation decisions are made or how influence is exercised.

Evan has reviewed a number of indices that illustrate the measurement of control in industrial organisations. These include, span of control; the number of levels of hierarchy; the ratio of administrative to production personnel; "time-span of discretion," which is defined as "the maximum length of time an employee is authorized to make decisions on his own initiative which commit a given amount of the resources of the organisation"; the hierarchical level at which given classes of decisions are made; and the formal limitations that apply to the decision-making authority of management. Some of these measures have been formulated to meet the requirements of particular conceptual schemes; others have been chosen for research, because they are readily available.

4 The Effective Organisation

What is efficiency in an Organisation?

Organizations exist to serve a variety of purposes, and the effective organization is one that get things done in such a way as to meet all of its objectives. In manufacturing industry the purpose is to produce sufficient goods of an appropriate specification, quality and price.

It is common practice to talk about the 'efficiency' of production. This normally means the relationship between the cost of the inputs and the value of the outputs—a ratio. But is an organization is to serve its purposes, whatever they may be, it needs to know more about what it is aiming to achieve, say than, hopefully, that it would like to be 99.9% efficient.

Once it is decided what it wants to make, and that it has got an appropriate product, an organization needs to meet certain operational objectives. These may be simply stated as:

- achieve output targets
- make products of appropriate quality
- be efficient, making full use of all of its resources, and

- operate in such a way as to ensui e survival.

Writers on the subject of management studies have drawn attention to the fact that in organizations there may be multiple goals. They stress the need to stand back and look at the organization as a whole, as well as individual parts of it, and to take a longer term view as well as short term one. Even at the crude level of the above objectives, we can see that there are bound to be these multiple goals, and we have only to look below the surface of each of these to begin to reveal may 'sub goals'.

For example, to achieve output targets we have to have the appropriate tools, machinery and materials, and sufficient numbers of the right kind of employee, properly trained, and who will regularly be available to do the work. they will also need to be well motivated to produce the required output of good quality goods!

If we then considered *how* all of this might be achieved we would begin to generate a long list of further sub goals, and the functions and tasks which need to be performed in order to meet this objective.

To 'be efficient' implies making full use of all of the resources. This should mean not only proper utilization of equipment and materials but also proper utilization of people. In the conventional concept of the term 'efficient', the proper use of people us often seen as 'keeping them at it'. We are often preoccupied with how *hard* people are working, perhaps paying too little attention to *what* they are given to do. As was suggested in the previous chapter, many employees are potentially capable of contributing more in the way of knowledge, talents, experience, skill and goodwill than their present work situation permits. It is just as wasteful to under-utilize the range and depth of peoples' capabilities as it is to have them standing idle, and the consequences for them and for the organization may be even worse.

If we consider the need of an organization to ensure its own survival the simple of 'efficiency' is really put into perspective. It is obvious that it is no use continuing to make products, however efficiently, which people are no longer willing to buy, nor is it sensible to rely on a material, the source of which is drying up. Similarly, it may not be appropriate to continue operating on the assumption that sufficient numbers of people will be available to do the work in the way that it has always been expected it would be done.

Even if survival is not obviously threatened, the really effective organization tries to keep in touch with the reality of its situation. It has the capacity to adapt and maintain itself as changes occur in the environment or in any of the variables with which it has to cope - products, technology, customer expectations, employee expectations and capabilities, and so on.

The nature of an organization

We have noted that the nature of the environment in which most activities exist is changing very rapidly. It is equally self-evident that an organization which exists in what has been called a 'turbulent' environment needs to be structured and managed differently to one which enjoys a relatively stable and predictable existence. But how? Different in what way?

Burns and Stalker are two social scientists who carried out studies in twenty firms in England and Scotland, with the support of the Scottish Council and the Department of Scientific and Industrial Research. The results of their studies, and their conclusions, were published in 1961 in their book 'The Management of Innovation'. All twenty studies were concerned with the question of what happens when new and unfamiliar tasks confront industrial concerns which are organized for relatively stable conditions. Most of the firms were in the electronics industry, and at the time of the study were subject to many new activities and continuous technical innovation.

Contrasting types of structure

One of the conclusions of this study was that there are two contrasting forms of organization and management system. One which they called mechanistic; this they saw as being appropriate to stable conditions. The other they called organic, that is one which is appropriate to changing conditions, ie those which give rise constantly to fresh problems, and unforeseen requirements for action. They identify and discuss a large number of features which characterize each form and these may be briefly stated as follows:

a) *Mechanistic Systems.* These are characterized by the breaking down of the tasks of the organization. Each task and functional role is precisely defined. There is a strict hierarchy, each level being responsible for the tasks carried out in the level immediately below, and answerable to the level immediately above. Communication and control tends to be vertical, an accordance with the hierarchy, the ultimate divisions being made at the top, where all wisdom is assumed to reside. There is an insistence on loyalty to the concern and obedience to superiors.

One can recognize here the bureaucratic, scientific management approach, with a highly structured organization, where many employees have limited tasks which are precisely defined. The situation in which this would be at its most appropriate would be a very *static*, ie an unchanging one. It ought to be possible to predict technology, products, processes, methods, product market, labour market, etc, and to make firm plans for an unvarying, uninterrupted flow of work. It is also based on an assumption that people prefer simple, undemanding jobs, or that they lack the competence to do more difficult ones.

b) *Organic System.* In this system jobs are not precisely defined, but can changes as conditions change. Individuals contribute any special knowledge or experience which they have to the common tasks of the concern, and responsibilities get distributed on this basis rather than on 'position'. Communication tends to be lateral, but even when people are of different rank it resembles consultation rather than command. Commitment to the concern's tasks is more highly valued than loyally or obedience.

The approach here would therefore be a flexible and adaptable one, with jobs which are more comprehensive, and which allow a high level of employee discretion. The situation in which this would be at its most appropriate would be a varying, unpredictable, unstable one. Collaborative working would replace the rigid divisions of functional demarcation. There would be an assumption that people need to do meaningful work which makes good use of their skills and abilities.

The two forms are seen to be at the ends of a spectrum of possibilities, so that in appropriate circumstances intermediate degrees of the mechanistic - organic ways of organizing work could be used, or both simultaneously in different parts of the organization. If follows that there is no single set of principles for good organization, but there is a need to be sensitive to the conditions which exist, and the changes which are occurring, and to adapt to appropriate management systems.

In other words, the organization, its structure and practices, has an impact on how people behave. If it is restrictive and bureaucratic it will get a limited response.

Many other students of organization have concluded that for an organization to be effective the needs, expectations and objectives of employees have to be integrated with the needs, expectations and objectives of the organization.

We have noted above that motivation is to do with getting commitment, and that the style of the relationships between the members of an organization is important for effectiveness. These relationships are closely concerned with organization structure—that is whether it is highly structured and rigid or adaptive and flexible. Finally, of course, all of these have implications for the design of the individual jobs which employees have to do. Developments in work structuring, job enrichment and the improvement of satisfaction at work have for the most part been directed at the individual job, and there is no doubt that much useful work has and can be done at this level. But individual jobs do not exist in isolation, and even if we start with them we will quickly be faced with the implications for the organization structure, the style of management - employee relationships. and the methods used to motivate employees.

An effective organization, seeking to make changes which will make jobs more meaningful and satisfying, whilst it maintains or improves its effectiveness, should seek to have a co-ordinated policy. This is essential if the desired results are to be achieved, and if they are to be more than occasional experiments, which only result in superficial changes in the details of the work task.

5 Organising

Why organise?

Any grouping or collection of people who are trying to work together to achieve a given objective, be it a number of soldiers trying to win a battle or a number of building operatives and craftsmen trying to build a house, work more effectively and quickly and have more chance of achieving their objective, if they are organized correctly.

Without organisations, modern day life quickly degenerate into near chaos. We depend on organisations to bring our food to the local supermarket, to supply petrol to the pumps at the local garage, to educate our children and to look after us when we are sick. We are part of an organisation in our working lives, while at home the family, that oldest organisation of all, has stood the lest of time and change and still survives, loved and cherished by most of us.

Organisations and organizing are so much part and parcel of our lives that we accept the concept of organizing without a second thought. Organizing means whatever resources are available -people, time, money, equipment, services etc.—to achieve objectives. For some people this may not mean much more than organizing their time throughout the day. Manager, however, control substantial resources, and they have to learn how to organize employees and organisations.

For managers the organizing function is made more difficult by the fact that much of their time is spent organizing people, and people change, daily, hourly, even by the minute. Managers are therefore constantly making adjustments to their organisations to cater for such things as the sickness of a key employee, an unexpected resignation, or the shortage of some key component because of a strike in a supplier's factory.

Some of the advantages of organisations were considered during our discussion of types of organisations. We noted, for example, that a partnership could draw on a wider range of expertise and greater financial resources than a one man business, Organisations are also social units; help and advice are provided to the members of the group, worries are shared, and the chances of success are improved when people from different backgrounds, ages and skills work in unison towards an agreed objective.

It is this basic need for human contact, to relate to other people and to have a greater chance of achieving success in any activity, that gives rise to the desire to organize and be organized. We may all be 'loners' occasionally, but we only reach our full potential as part of an organisation, however small. Management is about maximizing potential and management is therefore about organizing.

Principles of organisation

Spans of control

There will always be a limit to the number of manager can effectively control. Some management experts feel that six eight people is the maximum; others have suggested a smaller number. The appropriate span of control will depend on a variety of factors. First, are the subordinates qualified to make decisions without having to constantly refer upwards to the manager? Have they the skills and experience required to take the right course of action and see it through? Second, is the manager concerned prepared to delegate authority to his subordinates? Is this desirable for the manager's own career progression, or is it possible he might delegate himself out of a job? Third, a manager can supervise more people if the organisation has a well-defined planning function and agreed set of objectives, than if the objectives are vague or not widely understood.

Similarly, where an organisation has well developed, tried and tested communication systems that feed information quickly, to and from senior management, each manager is able to control a larger number of people. Indeed this may be the primary benefit of the modern communications and information systems discussed.

Finally, some organisations, particularly those in the public sector, depend a great deal on personal contact to operate effectively. These types of organisations will inevitably have small spans of control and involve many levels of subordinates and co-ordinates, the hallmark of a bureaucratic type of organisation.

Unity of objectives

Whatever the organisation structure finally decided upon, all parts of the organisation should work towards common objectives. In these days of international competition and scarce resources no manager can afford the luxury of parts of the organisation 'doing their own thing'. This is particularly true of labour-intensive organisations in the public sector and the service industries in the private sector, where the human resource plays such a key role.

As noted above, people are more likely to pursue the organisation's objectives rather than their personal interests if these objectives are clearly defined and widely understood. Unfortunately, experience shows that in public sector organisations 'politics' often leads to objectives being blurred or constantly changed, with consequential loss of efficiency.

Delegation

As noted during our discussion of the span of delegation implies that a senior manager gives discretion to a subordinate. Successful delegation requires that attention should be given to the following factors. First, adequate authority must be given to the subordinate to carry out the task. if a junior manager is given the job of running the mailroom, it should be made clear that he has authority over the mailroom staff and can specify the timing of the collection and delivery of the mail.

In situations like this, specifying the limits of authority is often easy. It is much more difficult where a senior manager has only a vague idea of what he wants and gives only broad and general instructions to a subordinate. In this situation there is much more likely to be a dispute later on as to whether the junior manager has exceeded his authority. Consider the situation in which a senior manager asks a subordinate to prepare a report on the feasibility of a proposed new product. The manager feels that a satisfactory report could be prepared as the basis of internal discussions with the production manager, personnel director etc. But the subordinate feels it necessary to obtain information about competitors products and therefore asks the market research department to undertake a survey. Two obvious sources of conflict arise. First, the market research staff may refuse to do what the junior manager requests.Second, if they do accept his authority and undertake the work, the senior manager may complain because of the costs involved.

Second, and following from the previous point, tasks delegated must be properly assigned, i.e. the subordinate must understand what is involved, accept the delegated discretion and know that his position and authority are not duplicated elsewhere in the organisation.

Finally, responsibility for the discretion delegated cannot be greater than the authority delegated, e.g. if a manager gives a subordinate the authority to sell certain items, that subordinate cannot be held responsible for high rates of breakage and customer complaints due to a bad design or faulty manufacturing.

Most successful managers are happy to delegate. They see it as being helpful to themselves and their organisations for a variety of reasons:

1 By delegating one can see which subordinates are likely to be 'high flyers', suitable for promotion, and which have reached the limit of their competence.

2 Delegation can provide a useful training tool, in that it enables managers to develop their potential. This may mean that junior managers are given discretion even though they do not perform as well as their seniors in the early stages. As they learn from experience and gain confidence their performance is likely to improve, and senior managers are often pleasantly surprised at how successful subordinates can be, given time and encouragement in undertaking tasks previously thought to be the preserve of the senior manager or 'the boss'.

3 All managers and individuals do some things better than others. If a subordinate is particularly skilled in some tasks it makes sense for a senior manager who may see these tasks as a 'bit of a chore', to let the junior manager do it. The tasks are likely to be performed more effectively and the senior manager will be able to spend more time on tasks for which he is better fitted.

4 Where an organisation is spread out geographically, e.g. with a headquarters and a number of area offices, it may be wise to delegate certain functions to junior managers in the area offices who are in closer touch with customers and the general public.

Whatever degree discretion a senior manager eventually decides to give to his subordinates the general principle is clear cut. Senior managers should concentrate their timed and effort on the major issues facing their organisations. Most senior managers are overworked, with more calls on their time than the working day allows for. Delegation of tasks to subordinates wherever possible makes good business and managerial sense. The tasks will often be done more cheaply, employee job satisfaction will be increased, and senior managers will be more effective.

The 'scalar' principle

In any organisation some individual must take ultimate authority and responsibility for the actions of that organisation. The more clear-cut is the line of authority between this individual and all the subordinate positions within the organisation, the more effective will be the decisionmaking process and the greater the organisation's efficiency. This unbroken line of responsibility between all individuals in an organisation is known as the 'scalar' principle. Unless the chain of command is clearcut people will not 'know where they stand', i.e. to whom they are responsible and to whom they refer matters beyond their own authority. Unity of command

Where an individual has responsibility to one clearly defined superior, the less likely it is that he will receive conflicting instructions. He is also likely to obtain more job satisfaction and a greater sense of purpose and responsibility in carrying out instructions, than if he is responsible to two or more superiors. The bigger the organisation, the more specialists it employs, the more difficult it is observe this 'unity of command' principle, with consequent adverse effects on morale and efficiency. For example a personnel officer may be asked by the production manager to provide additional workers; to meet this instruction may conflict with recruitment and induction procedures laid down by the personnel manager.

Types of organisation structure

There are two types of organisation structure, which exist side by side.

The formal organisation

This is the organisation structure designed by senior management to achieve the objectives of the organisation. It is the network of communication, responsibilities and groupings of individuals, that is seen by senior management as being the most effective. This network is often depicted in an organisation chart.

As mentioned previously, formal organisation structures are constantly modified by managers in response to a variety to a variety of pressures. Nevertheless it takes times time for a new structure to become fully operational, for all the relevant parts of the formal organisation to be re-organized, and for all the relationships to be modified.

The informal organisation

Within very organisation, alongside the formal organisation structure there exists the informal structure. This is based on relationships between individuals and groups and as such is much more dynamic and less easily definable than the more rigid formal structure. The 'old boy network', the 'office grapevine'; a temporary liaison between two sections to gain a working advantage over a third, e.g. sales and marketing versus production, are all examples of informal relationships.

In many ways, these informal organisations, because they reflect the present, real world situation, rather than what managers think the situation is, more powerful than the formal organisational links. If the two structures seriously diverge, it may become necessary to formalize at least some of the informal relationships; otherwise communication channels may break down and managers' freedom of action become curtailed. However, it is usually undesirable to try to suppress all informal relationships, since they can sometimes help to lubricate the formal machinery and make the organisation a more interesting place in which to work.

Levels within an organisation

Each organisation has its own individual number of levels, determined by an amalgamation of all the issues discussed in this chapter. But most organisations contain certain levels within the hierarchical structure, with clearly defined functions. At the top there are a few senior managers making policy decisions. At the bottom there are a much larger number of employees carrying out the detailed work of the organisation at the 'sharp end' so to speak. In the middle are the co-ordinators, planners and sectionheads controlling their particular functions, referring issues to senior management and receiving instructions back. The organisational hierarchies of typical public and private sector organisations are depicted.

It will be seen that the hierarchy at the public sector organisation is more complex because of the political element involved. Ratepayers and politicians take a much keener interest in the running of a local authority and are much likely to change their views—with consequent effects on the organisation—than the shareholders of a private company. The bureaucratic organisation and management structure tends to operate so as to deaden and soften the impact of political change in order to aid the organisation's survival and facilitate its management.

Private sector organisations reflect the impact of external changes more quickly and more fully, mainly because the implications of a change are less extreme. Although a loss o. sales is a serious matter, it would usually lead to fewer changes in policy than would a change from Conservative to Labour control of a large county council, especially if the political views of the council were not tempered by the advice of permanent officers.

Centralization versus de-centralization

Many large organisations have to decide whether all major decisions, responsibility and authority, should be concentrated at head office or whether there should be wider 'power sharing' with, for example, some decisions being made in area offices, There is obviously a connection with delegation, but we are concerned here with the structure of an organisation as a whole, whereas delegation refers to the style of individual managers.

Centralization has a number of advantages:

1 Communication systems of all types are made easier by having people and departments alongside one another.

2 Services such as mail, photocopying, plan printing, filing, reception, telephone, canteen, car parking and other support services can be

provided on an overall, rather than departmental, basis. This will produce savings in staff and enable costs to be more closely controlled.

3 The corporate image of an organisation is improved when the organisation is situated in one location. We are all familiar with the Town Hall or County Hall as symbolizing the centre of administration in a town. The large new civic centres and old Victorian 'gothic-style' town halls add a touch of grandeur and dignity to the operation of local services in a way several smaller buildings scattered throughout an area would not.

4 Various aspects of security can be improved in a centralized location, although against this has to be offset the dangers inherent in having all one's eggs in one basket', e.g. all the organisation's could be destroyed in one fire or robbery.

5 It easier to manage the operation and people when everything is under one roof.

De-centralization has the advantage that it decision making 'where the action is.' The sales office on site at a housing estate, the social services area office, the local clinic and the local police station are all examples of de-centralization. These out-stations provide a local link with the people they serve and ease of access for consumers. They enable a local approach to problem solving to be combined with help and advice from a headquarters organisation.

De-centralization only works if the people in the various locations are giver adequate authority to make decisions, and responsibility proportional to the decision-making power of each individual is agreed and exercised at all levels of the organisation.

De-centralization works best when the headquarters provides advice or some specialist support to research activity and this is coupled with good communication systems, widely understood objectives, and control systems which are followed by all concerned.

On-line computer systems now allow constant contact between a network of area or branch office and the main information files at headquarters, and thus help to overcome one of the main problems associated with de-centralization. Previously if you went into your bank, building society or the gas showroom, and wanted detailed information about your finances or accounts, a long wait frequently ensued. Now the answer is immediately available on a visual display screen with print out.

The most advanced example of this is the police national computer linked to the DVLC at Swansea. When a car's registration number is fed into the computer, details of the car., and its owner, can be given in seconds to the patrolling policeman on the beat.

There is no right answer to the question: 'should one centralize or decentralize?' Each case must be treated on its merits and the light of local circumstances. However, it would appear that more and more larger organisations in both the public and the private sectors are taking heed of the maxim 'small is beautiful' associated with the late E.F.Schumacher and are running their operation with local offices, linked by modern communication systems to a small headquarters organisation that provides policy guidance and advice and specialist help when required. In this way modern advances in electronic communications enable organisations to satisfy the increasing demand by consumers for the personal touch in their dealings with businesses and the public sector.

Deparmentation

Having decided, or even before making the decision, on centralization or de-centralization every senior manager has to decide how to group the various activities and individuals within his organisation. This organizing function is known as departmentation, and the main forms of departmentation are outlined below.

By customer

Where an organisation has a very important customer who requires a particular type of product or standard of service, it makes sense to have a group which can concentrate on the needs of this customer, Advertising agencies have 'account executives' whose job it is to look after the interests of a particularly valuable client and co-ordinate their agencies' approach to the client. Many food manufacturers have 'key account executives' who negotiate terms with the chief buyers of the large grocery multiples.

By advertising channel

The use of the various media now requires specialist skills if they are to be fully utilized to the advantage of an organisation. The high cost of advertising time or space makes it worth an organisation's while to develop a co-ordinated approach to the media concerned in order to obtain the preferential rates available to bulk buyers.

By process or equipment

Organizing under one head or section the computer operations of an organisation, or a particular type of production process that requires specialist skills, makes for organisational as well as managerial efficiency. Maintenance is made easier and the relevant trade and management 'know how' can be concentrated in one area.

By service or product

The establishment of a group to provide specialist recruitment advice, or to oversee the development of an engine would be examples of this form of departmentation. This should result in the more efficient use of specialized resources and a more co-ordinated approach to outside individuals and pressures.

By function

Organizing the total resources of an organisation by specialist functions—sales, production, accounts-is common practice in most organisations and dose not really require further comment here. Suffice it to say that the more numerous and more specialized the various departments are, the more difficult is the task of senior management to co-ordinate and manage.

By geographical area

Most readers will be familiar with this type of departmentation. It is particularly common in dividing up an organisation's sales or marketing forces into say the Scottish region, Wales, Northern England, the Midlands and the Home Counties. Regional and local tastes and differences can be catered for in this way, and it also aids overall managerial control in very large organisations that have national or international markets.

By time

Organizing according to time scales, e.g. day and night shifts, makes sense where round the clock production, service, or monitoring systems are in operation, and where, over long time periods, the human response is limited in its operational capability.

By actual numbers

The armed forces departmentalize themselves on these lines, e.g.a platoon has 30-33 men in it, a brigade 3,000. Whether in the private sector or the public sector there often exists an optimum number of people to do a particular job; too few and the job folds up, too many and people are 'falling over one another' Dividing the workforce up by numbers on the basis of the 'span of control', discussed earlier, takes account of the need for people to identify within a group.

Organisational relationships

Whatever span control is chosen, whatever the of departments or groupings eventually decided upon, management has the choice of certain tried and tested organisational relationships within the organisational structure they finally decide upon.

Line relationships

This refers to the direct working relationships between the vertical levels of an relationship where authority flows from the departmental head to the deputy, to section head and eventually to the person who actually dose the job of work. The communication channels are clear, authority is agreed, and instructions and information flow down and up between the individuals concerned.

Staff relationships

Most textbooks refer to a 'staff' relationship as an advisory function in either a specialist or assistant type of position. This is true insofar as the personnel manager or a management services officer may be regarded as 'advisors' to line managers. But in many large organisations the different between the 'line' and 'staff' function is often less clear cut. In such organisations one often finds staff specialists who also have line responsibility over their own staff. For example the personnel manager or director would have a 'staff' relationship or advisory role to the managing director on personnel policy, but line responsibility over staff in the training, employment, recruitment and safety sections of his own personnel section.

The best guide to the reader in attempting to assess whether a position is 'line' or 'staff' is to remember that the ultimate test is based on the personal relationships, especially in terms of authority, between the individuals concerned and not by purely departmental or sectional activities.

In systems of 'corporate planning' or the 'management team' concept in local government, the two roles are often combined, e.g. the director of education will be acting as a 'line' manager when he comes to speak on educational matters to the other members of the management team, but will act in a 'staff' capacity or advisory role when, as a member of the corporate management team of authority, he criticizes some service aspect of the corporate plan or budget.

Functional relationships

This relationship occurs where a line manager delegates to an individual or section the authority to carry out particular processes, policies, operations etc. The function can be delegated to either other 'line' managers or 'staff' advisors and specialists. This form of delegation is especially common in situations which require a grouping of people and activities to do a particular job, e.g. the move to a new office building, the installation of a new computer or the setting up of a new grievances procedure. Once the job is completed the functional authority often ends and the staff concerned return to their normal work.

Committee relationships

We have already made reference to committees as a system of managing. Suffice it to say here that committees play a large part in organisational structures in both the public and private sectors. Indeed it is often said that they are part of the British way of life; if in doubt then set up a committee. Viewed as part of the organizing function, committees can either be formal, i.e. have written remit and authority to carry out a specific function, or informal or ad hoc, i.e. set up for some temporary purpose to act as a pressure release valve or as a 'sounding board' for management.

Organisation charts

(a) Vertical

(b) Horizontal

(c) Circular or concentric

(d) Flow

Working parties

In recent years the increasing need for participation and specialist advice has led to the setting up, particularly in the public sector, of a variant of the committee system, i.e. the working party.

The aim of a working party is to co-ordinate the specialist knowledge of various interested parties to solve a particular problem. This means that the relationships in a working party differ slightly from those in a committee. In principle in a working party the members contribute from their own specialist viewpoint and not as equal participants able to criticize everyone and everything as in a committee.

Matrix relationships

This type of organisational relationship was pioneered by the Americans in their space programme in the 1960s. It combines many of the relationships we have discussed and involves staff having a dual responsibility. First, they have a responsibility to their immediate superior. Second, they have a relationships to the specialist working group and the project team of which they are members. The aim of this structure is to obtain the benefits of multi-discipline project teams at middle management level and below, whilst allowing line managers at senior level control of their specific responsibilities, even though these may be spread over several projects.

Organisation charts

There are four main types of charts that are commonly used to project to depict the relationships in organisations.

Problems managers face when organizing

Organizing the resources under their control is one of the most difficult functions managers have to undertake and whatever the solution ultimately chosen, most managers will experience one, or combination, of the following problems.

1 The plans paid down by senior management are translated into imprecise, unachievable objectives that have not gained the commitment of the employees concerned.

2 Working relationships within the organisation are ill-defined, vague and exist only on an informal or very personal basis.

3 The degree of delegation is inadequate and inadequate authority is given to those to whom responsibility is delegated.

4 Communication systems are inadequate with the result that management does not really know what is going on or is unaware of the true feelings of the workforce.

5 A breakdown occurs in the chain of command, such as the mixing up of line and staff relationships, the granting of functional authority without responsibility, bad supervision.

6 A period of rapid change leads to constant re-organisations so that the whole structure is in a state of flux, and no one has time to adapt to and fully implement organisational changes.

Experienced managers will recognize the above symptoms and take steps to rectify the situation. In many cases the above issues are the results of 'people problems' and can only be solved by re-training and management development, or at the worst, removal of the individual concerned.

6 Control, Performance, and Satisfaction

The present investigation is concerned with the relationship between organizational effectiveness and social control in organizations. In particular, it is designed to explore two aspects of control: the *distribution* of control among organizational levels, and the *bases* for this control.

In many discussions of organizational life there appears to be a serious dilemma concerning control. On the one hand, hierarchical control is said to be necessary to insure efficient administration and coordination of effort. On the other hand, decentralization of control and decision making is said to lead to higher rank-and-file motivation. Recent research has suggested that his may not really be a dilemma. It has been argued that increased control at the lower level need not, and should not, involve any sort of proportionate decrease in control at some other level. A number of studies indicate that relatively high amounts of control exercised by members at *all* organizational echelons is associated with higher performance and increased satisfaction. Tannenbaum and Likert have argued that this pattern of high total control is successful because it involves members at all levels of the organization, leading to more effective decisions and also to higher motivation.

Likert and Tannenbaum have suggested that the processes underlying a system of high control and its effects derive essentially from the satisfaction of the ego motives of the individuals, such as the desire for status achievement, and acceptance. If their interpretation is correct, then we would expect reward, referent, and expert power to be the more important bases underlying total control and its implications. In contrast, if the more traditional Weberian view is indeed correct, then the more important bases of control and its effects would be legitimate authority and the manipulation of rewards and sanctions.

The setting for the present study has certain features which make it especially attractive for our purposes. It involves subjects in responsible positions, with fairly high levels of skill and income. Thus we have an opportunity to see whether earlier findings obtained largely from rank-and-file workers can be generalized to persons at higher organizational level. Another important advantage is the availability of accurate individual performance data, which permits us to study factors affecting performance at individual as well as group levels. Finally, the subjects are located in 36 branch offices, each under the supervision of an office manager. We are thus able to study a fairly large number of distinct organizational units, each with basically the same tasks and the same criteria of success.

Some methodological considerations

Frequently, quantitative studies of organizations depend upon members' perceptions to provide measures of organizational characteristics, particularly administrative characteristics. Indeed, most of the research mentioned above falls into this category. The traditional procedure for handling such data is to characterize each organizational unit in terms of average ratings by all respondents in that unit. Thus, for example, if a researcher found that organizational units with high mean ratings of total amount of control also have relatively high mean satisfaction ratings, he might well conclude that total control and satisfaction are positively related at the organizational level. More specifically, he might view the pattern of influence as a part of the objective *structure* of the organizational environment which has real-life consequences for its members.

While organizational studies using this traditional form of analysis have been valuable, they continue to be subject to a serious weakness: what appears to be an objective structure effect may in fact be spurious-merely a reflection of purely individual-level relationship. Returning to our example, a positive correlation between mean satisfaction and mean ratings of total control might indicate only that persons who *perceive* a high degree of total control tend also to be satisfied persons. Such an individual-level relationship would be consistent with a *phenomenological* interpretation of the control-satisfaction findings.

Tannenbaum and Smith studied the problem of structural versus phenomenlogical effects using several analytic techniques in addition to the correlation of group mean data. They concluded that both types of effect occurred in their study, depending upon the criterion used to measure organizational effectiveness. When the criterion was the amount of time spent in organizational affairs, a structural relationship with patterns of control was observed. But in the case of loyalty, a more subjective dimension, a phenomenological effect appeared.

The analysis strategy used in the present study, following the same basic approach as Tannenbaum and Smith, makes an operational distinction between office-level effects and individual-level effects. We assume that the criterion scores (performance and satisfaction) *for each individual* are influenced in part by aspects of the organizational environment which are common to most or all of his office colleges, and we refer to these influences as *office-level effects.* Such effects include, but are by no means limited to, the impact of administrative characteristics such as control and bases of power. We assume that the criterion scores are also influenced by a host of idiosyncratic factors which differ from person to person, and we refer to these influences as *individual-level effects.* This definition includes so-called phenomenological effects, but it also includes such spurious relationships as halo effects and simple response biases. Note that the same *individual* criterion scores are used to assess both office-level and individual-level effects; we are thus exploring the extent to which each subject's performance and satisfaction are affected by office-level versus individual-level variables.

Ideally, of course, office-level variables should be manipulated experimentally, measured by observers, or assessed through other methods which are independent of the persons directly involved. In the present study, however, it was necessary to rely on the subjects' own perceptions. Nevertheless, we have been able to maintain the distinction between office-level and individual-level effects in the analysis of our results. Our basic strategy is to partial out the individual's own perception of office characteristics and compare his performance and satisfaction with the perceptual measures of the other group members. And we consider this distinction to be an important advance over the traditional correlation of group mean data.

Method

Research site

The data used in the present study were obtained in 36 branch offices of a national firm selling intangibles. Each branch office is managed by a single office manager, who has sole responsibility for the conduct of his office. His functions include supervision, on-the-job training of employees, and enforcement of home-office polices.

Directly under each office manager are a number of salesmen. The salesman's functions include soliciting and opening new accounts, and servicing existing accounts; he may also serve as the client's main source of information and expertise for decisions leading to sales. Since the firm derives its income largely from commissions on the sale of intangibles, the salesman is the basic producer in any branch office. The salaries of salesmen are indirectly related to individual productivity; most are within a range from $10,000 to $25,000 per year.

The remaining employees in each branch office serve in essentially a supporting or staff capacity. They provide necessary technical information, secretarial and clerical services, and the like, which help the salesmen provide service to their clients. In the present study we will not deal directly with these staff functions; instead, we will concentrate on the line side of the branch office: the officer manager and his salesmen.

The branch offices used in the analysis were divided into two groups for separate analysis. The 18 offices in Group A are all located in areas judged to have high business potential, and yet they vary widely in actual office performance. Offices in Group B are located in areas rated as having lower business potential, and yet some are high on actual performance, others relatively low. Ratings of business potential were derived from the pooled judgment of 10 high-level members of the home-office staff who had personal knowledge of the business conditions. The 18 offices in Group

A were selected from among those offices which at least 8 of the 10 raters placed in the top quartile for business potential. The 18 offices in Group B were selected from among those which at least 8 rates placed *below* the top quartile. Thus in terms of business potential, the Group A offices may be more homogeneous than the Group B offices.

In order to restrict the sample to those offices having continuity of operations and leadership, no office was included which had been established within the 5-year period preceding the study, or which had experienced a change of manager within the 2 years preceeding the study.

Measures

The data for this study consist of sales performance measures and salesmen's questionnaire responses. The number of salesmen in Group A offices ranged from 10 to 35, with a mean of 23.4 and median of 22.5. In Group B the number ranged from 8 to 17, with a mean of 13.1 and median of 14. The total number of respondents was 656, with 421 in Group A offices and 235 in Group B offices.

Virtually every salesman in each of the 36 offices filled out an extensive questionnaire dealing with many aspects of his work and his adjustment to it.

The administrative variables of interest in the present study include control, and the bases of the office manager's power. The criterion variables consist of salesmen's performance, and their satisfaction with their office manager.

Control

Two closely related measures of control were used. They have been treated separately because they involved somewhat different "influence receivers." The measures of *control over the office* dealt with the general amount of influence over the way the office is run. The *interpersonal control* measures dealt strictly with influence patterns between the office manager and his salesmen.

The following questionnaire item was used as a measure of the office manager's control over the office: "In general, how much say or influence do you feel has on how your office is run?" The extent of salesmen's control over the office was measured by a similar item: "In general, how much say or influence do you feel [the salesmen as a group] have on how your office is run?" Response categories for both items ranged from 1, "little or no influence," to 5, "a great deal of influence." A measure of *total control over the office* was derived by combining the responses to these two items.

The following items were used to measure the amount of interpersonal control between the office manager and his salesmen: "How much say or influences does your office manager have with when it comes to activities and decisions that affect the performance of your office? Now, thinking in the other direction, how much say or influence in your office have on your office manager when it comes to his activities and decisions that affect the performance of your office?" Both items used response categories ranging from 1, "no influence at all," to 5, "a great deal of influence." A measure of *total interpersonal control* was derived by adding the responses to the two items.

Bases of power

A single questionnaire item was used to asses five bases of the office manager's power or influence over the salesman respondent: referent, expert, reward, coercive, and legitimate power.

Listed below are five reasons generally given by people when they are asked *why* they do the things their superiors suggest or want them to do. Please read all five carefully. Then number them according to their importance to you as reasons for doing the things your office manager suggests or wants you to do. *Give rank "I" to the most important factor, "2" to the next, etc.* "I do the things may office manager suggests or wants me to do because:

A. "I admire him for his personal qualities, and want to act in a way that merits his respect and admiration;

B. "I respect his competence and good judgment about things with which he is more experienced than I;

C. "He can give special help and benefits to those who cooperate with him;

D. "He can apply pressure or penalize those who do not cooperate:

E. "He has a legitimate right, considering his position, to expect that his suggestions will carried out."

In order to simplify analysis and interpretation of results, the rank values for this item were later reversed so that a value of 5 indicate maximum importance. I indicates minimum importance. The measures of the five bases of power are not independent, because of the ranking procedure involved; in a sense, any single base of power can be given prominence only at the expense of the other bases.

Satisfaction with office manager

Each salesman's satisfaction with his office manager was assessed by the following item: "All things considered, how satisfied are you with the way your office manager is doing his job? Response categories ranged from 1, "very dissatisfied," to 5, "very satisfied."

Standardized salesman performance

The measure of salesmen's performance was designed to rule out the effects of length of service upon dollar productivity, thus permitting a fair comparison of younger men with more experienced men. This was accomplished by separating salesmen into the following subgrouping based on years of experience: less than 1 year, 1-2 years, 2-3 years, 3-4 years, 4-5 years, 5-10 years, and more than 10 years. Within each of these subgroups, the distribution of dollar productivity was sharply skewed toward the high end. A logarithmic transformation applied to the dimension of dollar productivity yielded distributions that were approximately normal. Moreover, although the means of each of the seven subgroups were different, the standard deviations of the transformed distributions were almost identical. Each sales man assigned a score corresponding to his position within the transformed productivity distribution for his subgroup. The standard performance scores which resulted from these operations were independent of length of service and approximated the normal distribution.

Significance level

Because many of the relationships examined this study were not specifically predicted n advance, two-tailed test were used with the .05 minimum criterion for significance.

Statistical analysis and rationale

Our analysis explores the effects of several administrative character upon two criterion variable, performance and satisfaction. The mean responses and standard deviations for all measures are presented.

We make the assumption that the best available estimate of organizational structure in our data is a composite of perceptions within a given organizational unit. Thus our measure of each administrative characteristic consists of the mean rating by all salesmen in a given office. These mean ratings are correlated with performance and satisfaction at two distinct levels of analysis: office mean criterion scores and individual criterion sources.

Office mean criterion scores

The first level of analysis involves what we have

called the traditional comparison of office mean data. The correlations between administrative characteristics and office mean criterion scores are presented. This form of analysis often highlights office-level effects, since may kinds of individual-level effects may be canceled by the use of mean criterion data. We noted earlier, however, that *systematic* individual-level effects, including some phenomenological effects, are not canceled, and the danger that they will be misinterpreted as genuine office-level effects remains a major weakness of the traditional method. Thus the analysis cannot stand alone as a demonstration of office-level effects; further evidence is necessary.

Individual criterion scores

The second level of analysis deal with individual salesmen; presents correlations computed between administrative characteristics and the individual criterion ratings. This form of analysis deals with the question: Given the many causes of an individual's performance and satisfaction, what is the relative importance of administrative characteristics such as the distribution and bases of control?

Isolation of office-level effects

The individual level of analysis has an additional advantage; it can tell us something about the *way* in which administrative characteristics have their influence on individual performance and satisfaction. Early in this paper we raised the question: Is it merely the *perception* of these characteristics which effects the criterion variables. In order to deal with this issue, the relationships are presented in two forms: zero-order correlations and partial correlations. The partial correlations rule out the effects of each salesman's own perception of the office administrative characteristics, thereby removing that portion of the relationships, which might be attributed to individual-level effects. The relationships that remain are office-level effects. We interpret these office-level relationships as being specific structural effects of control and bases of power, since these are the office-level variables we have attempted to measure.It must be noted, however, that this particular interpretation does not follow necessarily from the logic of our analysis. It is possible, for example, that our measures have actually tapped some cultural stereotype common to the office as a whole, rather than the actual behaviors assumed to be associated with control and bases of power.

Effects office administration characteristics

Control

Measures of control over the office and interpersonal control correlated positively with both criterion measures. These positive relationships appeared no matter who exercised the control—the office manager, the salesmen, or both. Moreover, there is a strong positive relationship between the amount of interpersonal control exercised by the office manager and that exercised by the salesmen. These findings seem inconsistent with the position that the total amount of control in any situation remains a fixed quantity; on the contrary, they support the view that the total amount of control or influence is variable.

Bases of power

For the average salesman, the most important basis of the office manager's control was legitimate power, nevertheless, in offices relatively high on this dimension, respondents indicated significantly less satisfaction with their office manager, and there was a tendency for performance to be lower.

The second and third most important dimensions were expert and referent power. Offices in which the office manager was rated relatively high on these bases of power were also high on performance and satisfaction with the office manager.

Reward and coercive power were rated the least important reasons for complying with the office manager's wishes, and both were negatively related to the criterion variables.

It is important to note that the five bases of power related to the overall amount of control in much the same way as they related to performance and satisfaction: Correlations with total control were .66 and .58 for expert and referent power; -.48, -.49, and -.58 for legitimate, reward, and coercive power, respectively. Nearly identical correlations were obtained with the measure of total interpersonal control.

Some caution must be exercised in interpreting correlations with the bases of power.

The ranking method used in obtaining the data makes it impossible for all five bases of power to be correlated in the same direction with any single criterion variable. Thus, it may be that positive correlations with expert and referent power are responsible for negative correlations with the other bases of power, or vice versa.

Office-level versus individual-level effects

A comparison of the zero-order and partial correlations indicates the presence of office-level relationships between the administrative characteristics and both criterion variables. When the effects of the individual's perception of administrative characteristics are removed, the small but significant correlations with performance are not reduced. On the other hand, the same partial correlation procedure does lead to a substantial reduction in the correlations between administrative characteristics and satisfaction with the office manager. This suggests that a portion of the zero-order relationship with satisfaction is attributable to individual-level effects.

Isolation of individual effects

In order to isolate individual-level effects, it is necessary to reverse the strategy employed earlier; we now rule out any possibility of an office-level effect, thus leaving only those relationships which we have defined as individual effects. This is accomplished by treating each office separately, and correlating individual perceptions of administrative characteristics with individual criterion scores. Since we are considering objective administrative characteristics to be identical for all persons within a given office, these intraoffice correlations provide a measure of pure individual-level effects.

The pattern of relationships is clear and highly consistent. Individual performance is unrelated to individual perceptions of office administrative characteristics. On the other hand, an individual salesman's satisfaction with his office manager is significantly related to his personal appraisal of administrative characteristics in his office, and the pattern of individual-level relationships parallels very closely the pattern of office-level effects isolated earlier.

Relationship between performance and satisfaction

On the whole, our criterion variables-performance and satisfaction with the office manager—have shown fairly similar patterns of correlation with administrative characteristics. This finding might indicate that high performance causes a salesman to be satisfied with his office manager; or perhaps such satisfaction is a cause of high performance. If either of these explanations were correct, we should find that an *individual's* performance is correlated with his personal satisfaction with the manager. But in fact, when the possibility of office-level effects is removed, no such relationship is evident; the mean intraoffice correlation between performance and satisfaction is -.02. However, the correlation between office mean performance and office mean satisfaction is .35, $p<.05$. In other words, our criterion measures covary at the office mean level of analysis, but are entirely independent at the intraoffice level, and these findings are fully consistent with the view that performance and satisfaction are subject to similar but separate *structural* relationships, with the administrative characteristics under study.

7 Organisations in the Private and Public Sectors

Introduction

Having acquainted the reader with the concept of management, the functions of managers and the environment within which managers operate, we now consider the types of organizations within which managers work.

Britain has a mixed economy, i.e. it has both a private and a public sector. Most private sector organizations supply goods and services with the aim of making a profit. Some public sector organizations supply goods and services, while other undertake purely administrative activities. We discuss both sectors in turn, beginning with the larger, private sector.

Private sector organisations

About two thirds of all workers are found in the private sector. This sector comprises several types of organizations. There are about 1 million unincorporated business — one main businesses and partnerships, making this the most important type numerically.

The one man business

By far the most popular type of organization is the one man business or sole trader. They are especially common in agriculture, retailing and the provision of local services such as building repairs, plumbing, window cleaning etc. Because the business is owned by one person, the management style is usually compact and personal and the owner is able to exercise his entrepreneurial skills to the full, e.g. by branching out into new lines of business.

In practice, most sole traders keep to the business they know well and remain small. For example, the typical small trader in retailing has one shop which he runs on his own or with the help of his immediate family. However, there are some outstanding exceptions to this rule. For example, David Quayle opened his first D.I.Y. shop on his own, built up a large chain of shops by 1981, before going public. Shortly afterwards the chain was bought by Woolworths for a considerable sum of money making David Quayle a very rich man indeed.

The main source of funds for the one man business are the owner's savings and ploughed back profits. These are often sufficient, but may well be inadequate if the owner wishes to expand rapidly. He may be able to obtain short-term credit from his suppliers, and equipment on hire purchase. He is also likely to approach a bank for a loan or overdraft facilities, but the bank will probably require what it considers to be adequate collateral. The British banking system, is not well known for its entrepreneurial spirit, although in recent years it has modified its 'safe is sure' attitude.

The freedom to exercise the owner's entrepreneurial skills, noted above, may not be an unmixed blessing. In the early years of a business or when it is expanding, a wide range of managerial skills—financial, marketing, production etc.—may be required and these skills are seldom found to the same extent in one person. The danger is that in following his entrepreneurial nose, e.g. in finding new markets, the owner may disregard other areas that are equally vital to the health of the business, e.g. planning and controlling the cash flow. The successful owner-manager will recognize his weakness and obtain relevant advice—on a full or part-time basis—from others.

Even then the owner will probably have to work much longer hours—at least until the business is well established—than the average salaried manager. Shopkeepers often have to stock-take after the last customer has gone; farmers have to assess their needs for new machinery, fertilizer, seeds, and calculate the cost, after their 'working day' has ended.

Succession issues, i.e. what happens when the owner retires or dies, are also a cause for concern. Unless the business is to be sold as a going concern, future managers must be developed. It is sometimes said that a farmer should have sons or, if not, pretty daughters!

Partnerships

Partnerships are found mainly in the professions, e.g. doctors, dentists, lawyers, accountants. The partnership overcomes some of the problems faced by the one man business. First, capital is provided by all of the partners, who can be from two or twenty in number. As providers of capital the partners share the financial risk.

Second, and probably more important, the partnership allows the spreading of the workload and the ability to draw on additional expertise; for example a legal partnership will try to ensure that at least one partner is expert in each of the major branches of the law.

The partners' salary and share of profits will be distributed on an agreed basis. In the event of insolvency, however, all of the partners are liable to contribute to the payment of the partnership's debts, and this means that great attention must be paid to the management of the business, including the choice and number or partners.

Limited companies

The term 'limited' refers to the fact that the owners' liability is limited to the capital subscribed in the company.

There are several types of company:

Registered companies

The most popular type, these companies are registered in accordance with the Companies Acts.

Chartered companies

These are charitable bodies and other institutions that are granted a royal charter.

Statutory companies

These companies are found under a specific act of parliament.

Registered companies are by far the most important of the three types, there being almost 700,000 in Great Britain. They can be further divided into private companies and public companies which are much more important in terms of their aggregate size.

The main reason for the small size of the average private company is that the maximum number of shareholders is limited by law to 50. There is no limit to the number of shareholders in public companies. Moreover the securities of the larger public companies are quoted on the shock exchange, where they can be traded freely. This encourages small shareholders to buy shares, and companies such as I.C.I. and Marks and Spencer have many thousand shareholders..

Public companies operate in a wide range of industries: manufacturing, construction, retailing etc. The biggest usually operate in several industries and in a large number of countries. This means that their revenue is very substantial. In fact, the turnover of General Motors is greater than the national income of many countries.

The management of these large companies or groups of companies is a very complex task, and a

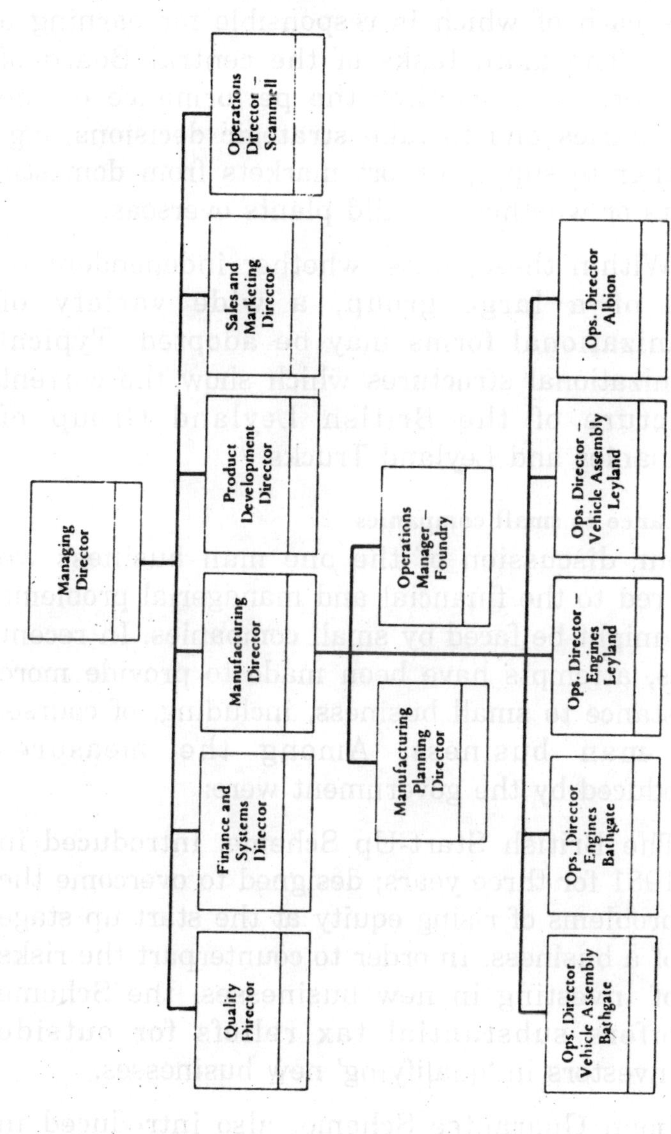

Figure: Leyland trucks, 1983. Reproduced by courtesy of British Leyland.

common way of making that task more manageable is to split the group into individual units each of which is responsible for earning a profit. The main tasks of the central Board of Directors is to monitor the performance of the subsidiaries and to take strategic decisions, e.g. whether to supply export markets from domestic plants or whether to build plants overseas.

Within these units, whether independent or part of a large group, a wide variety of organizational forms may be adopted. Typical organizational structures which show the current structure of the British Leyland Group of Companies and Leyland Trucks.

Assistance to small companies

In our discussion of the one man business we referred to the financial and managerial problems that might be faced by small companies. In recent years, attempts have been made to provide more assistance to small business, including, of course, one man business. Among the measures introduced by the government were:

1 The British Start-Up Scheme, introduced in 1981 for three years; designed to overcome the problems of rising equity at the start up stage of a business. In order to counterpart the risks of investing in new businesses, the Scheme offers substantial tax reliefs for outside investors in 'qualifying' new businesses.

2 Loan Guarantee Scheme, also introduced in 1981 for three years; under this Scheme the

government provides a guarantee for up to 80 per cent of a loan made by a bank.

Increasing public finance for small companies, especially in high technology industries, has also been made available through the National Enterprise Board.

The clearing banks - Lloyds, Barclays, etc. - have also become more willing than previously to lend to firms for longer periods, and a number of financial situations catering especially for small businesses have been established.

The government has also attempted to help small businesses by providing advice e.g. through the Small Firms Advisory Service, by giving tax concessions, and by attempting small firms from the Provision of some legislation, e.g. the Equal Opportunities Act.

Collective organizations

This final set of organizations straddles the private and public sectors, although in most instances the membership is to be found mainly in private sector organizations. The main aims of collective organizations are fist to link members in a group capable of exercising collective pressure, and second, to provide information, technical advice, training and other facilities that an individual member might not be able to afford on his own.

As we noted in the previous chapter some collective organizations, such as the Consumers' Association and Friends of the Earth, bring pressure to bear on business organizations. In this section we are *mainly* concerned with collective organizations that represent business organizations or their members in their dealings with other organizations and with government. There has been a considerable increase in the number and size of such collective organizations in recent years, for several reasons:

1 The tendency of governments to be more consultative in their approach to the private sector;

2 The growth and increased influence of public sector organizations at local level, calling for corresponding organized pressure from the private sector;

3 The need for greater technical advice and expertise, not within the financial resources of individual members.

Also, increased influence on the part of one collective organization may lead to the establishment or growth of an organization able to exert countervailing pressure, e.g. TUC and CBI.

The collective institutions that we are concerned with in this chapter can be classified as follows:

Business groups

The largest business group, the Confederation of British Industry, is the management equivalent of the TUC, in that it advises and consults with the government on a wide range of issues affecting employers. Firms in particular industries have formed employers' associations to negotiate with trade unions on wages, conditions of employment etc. These or other associations may also make representations to government concerning the level of imports, energy prices etc.

Chambers of Commerce and Chambers of Trade and are particularly concerned with local issues. They deal with local and regional authorities with regard, for example, to planning applications or the provision of local road or sewage facilities. However, this local focus may involve activities over a wide geographical areas, e.g. some Chambers arrange visits to export markets and entertain representatives of overseas companies which might build factories in the area.

Labour groups

The main objectives of unions are the projection and improvement of their members' positions, although they also enjoy a wider political interest. Unions may be organized on a 'craft' basis, e.g. ASLEF, an industry basis, e.g. the National Union of Mineworkers, or a more general basis, e.g. the Transport and General Workers Union. Most unions have officials on the stop floor who are responsible for day-to-day negotiations with management. There are generally local and district committees, co-ordinated by a national executive which usually has a rapid secretariat. The executive deals with matters of policy.

Most unions are affiliated to the Trade Union Congress, a body representing some 50 per cent of the whole workforce of the country. Each year a

Congress is held at which common policy aims are agreed. The Congress elects a Council which acts as its representative in consultations with the government and employers' associations.

Professional groups

These bodies control entry qualifications, lay down codes of conduct provide advice and act as a pressure group for their members' interests. Because of their expertise professional groups are often consulted by government on relevant matters, e.g. one would expect the government to consult the British Medical Association on matters affecting the operation of the National Health Service, or the British Institute of Management on matters affecting managers in all types of organizations.

Public sector organizations

The public sector comprises many different types of organization, and these can be classified in several ways, two of which are considered here.

First, one can make a distinction between the trading and non-trading sectors. The trading sector consists of organizations which supply goods and services at prices designed to cover their costs. This sector, which mainly comprises the nationalized industries, accounts for around 10 per cent of the total employed labour force. The non-trading sector has organizations which provide goods and services free or at highly subsidized prices, or which are simply engaged in administrative activities. This sector accounts for over 20 per cent of the employed labour force, especially important areas of employment being health and personal social services, education and the armed forces.

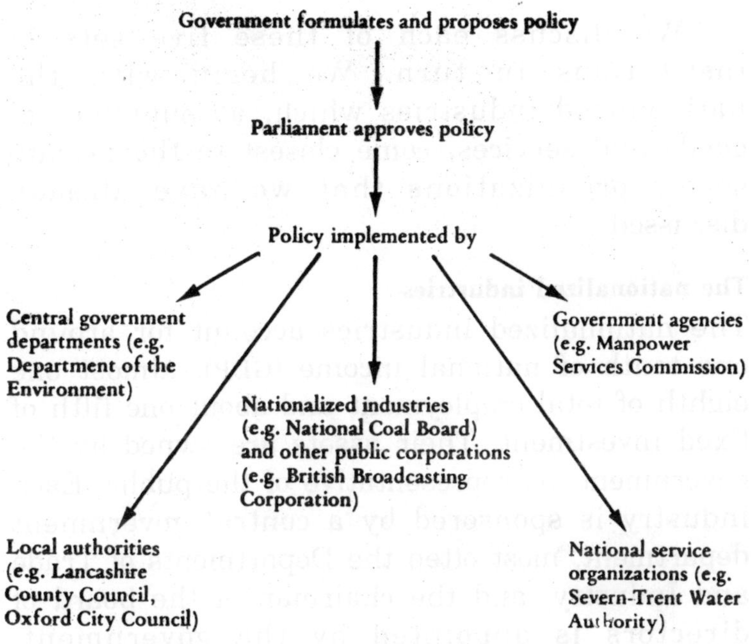

Public sector orgnisations: the policy process

An alternative classification follows what might be called the constitutional approach. It takes as its starting point the fact that all organizations in the public sector derive their authority from the Monarchy via Parliament. Parliament, as the supreme legislative authority, makes policy, largely by passing Bills introduced by the government. The government then has the responsibility for executing or implementing policy. It may decide that the implementation should be undertaken by central government departments, local authorities, nationalized industries, national service organizations or other government agencies.

We discuss each of these five sets of institutions in turn. We begin with the nationalized industries which, as suppliers of goods and services, come closest to the private sector organizations that we have already discussed.

The nationalized industries

The nationalized industries account for around one tenth of national income (GDP), almost one eighth of total employment and about one fifth of fixed investment. Their assets are owned by the government, as representative of the public. Each industry is sponsored by a central government department, most often the Departments of Trade and Industry, and the chairman of the board of directors is appointed by the government. However, the employees are *not* civil servants. The nationalized industries obtain the bulk of their revenue by the sale of the products at commercial prices. This means that, for example, the Post Office is a nationalized industry but the B.B.C., whose revenue is derived from licence fees, is not.

In terms of employment, the most important nationalized industries are the National Coal Board (284,000 workforce), British Telecom (247,000), Electricity (231,000), British Rail (227,000), the Post Office (185,000), British Steel Corporation (110,000) and British Gas (106,000).

From this it will be evident that the state has a major stake in the industrial base of the country. The principle underlying nationalization was that while Parliament should have the right to monitor the progress of the industries, e.g. by questioning Ministers from sponsoring departments, the industries would be free from ministerial interference on a day-to-day basis. In fact, ministers and civil servants have intervened in the industries' activities to a much greater extent than originally envisaged.

Intervention has meant that decisions are often taken on non-commercial grounds. The Central Electricity Generating Board has bought domestically produced coal rather than cheaper coal from abroad and has built coal rather than oil-burning power stations that were cheaper to run; British Airways has run unprofitable services to sparsely populated areas; the National Coal Board has kept open unprofitable pits in order to maintain employment.

This is not the place to discuss the merits of government intervention. The main point we wish to make here is that government intervention, and a mix of commercial and non-commercial objectives, adds to the difficulties faced by managers in the nationalized industries. It also means that senior managers spend a great deal of time consulting with their counterparts in the civil service, and so have less time to devote to the process of forward planning than senior managers in private sector organizations.

One area in which governments have frequently intervened in the prices set by the nationalized industries. At times, the government has refused to allow the industries to increase prices as much as they wished. Subsequently, as financial losses have been incurred, controls have been lifted and prices have risen at a faster rate than in the private sector. This erratic pattern of price changes creates problems for the purchasers of the industries' products and adds to management's difficulties.

Central government departments

The Central Government plays an increasing role in the day to day lives of the citizens of most developed countries. Total government spending often amounts to nearly fifty per cent of the Gross National Product. In the amounts to nearly fifty per cent of the Gross National Product. In the U.K., despite recent attempts by the Thatcher Government to limit government involvement in the day-to-day operation of organizations, the tide of central government influence shows little sign of retreating.

Although managers and organizations frequently seek more freedom to run their own affairs, they also demand government intervention; protection from cheap imports, or subsidies in difficult economic times, or government orders to protect jobs. At the same time there are increasing demands for more social and welfare facilities, for minimum standards of health and safety in factories, for better job protection and minimum standards of training. These and many other demands lead to an expansion of government influence and involvement.

It would not be appropriate in a book of this nature to attempt a comprehensive account of the activities of the central government. But to aid the reader's understanding we present a classification of government departments and outline their main areas of responsibility. Four broad areas of policy can be identified as shown in Figure.

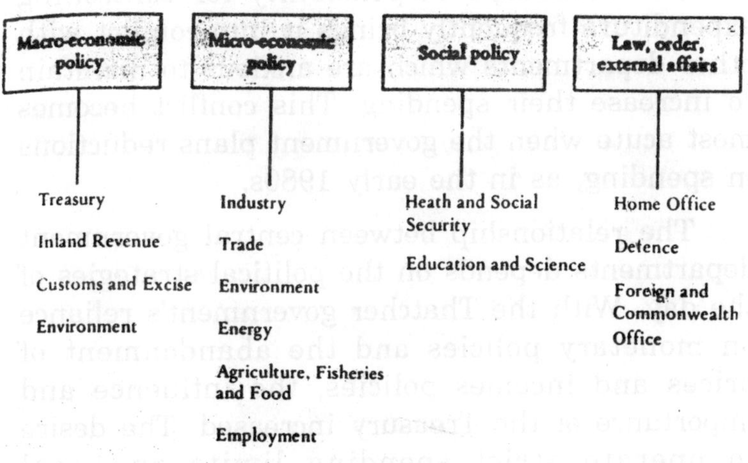

The main areas of responsibility of the major government jepartments.

Departments responsible for macro-economic policy

Macro-economic policy is designed to influence the behaviour of the economy as a whole, e.g. the rate of the inflation, the level of employment and unemployment. The Treasury is responsible for all aspects of macro-economic policy and its central role is recognized by the fact that the Prime Minister is its formal head, although the Chancellor of the Exchequer acts as its head on a day-to-day basis.

The basis of the Treasury's power is its responsibility for the raising of finance and government expenditure.

The Treasury's responsibility for controlling expenditure frequently brings it into conflict with other departments which are anxious to maintain to increase their spending. This conflict becomes most acute when the government plans reductions in spending, as in the early 1980s.

The relationship between central government departments depends on the political strategies of the day. With the Thatcher government's reliance on monetary policies and the abandonment of prices and incomes policies, the influence and importance of the Treasury increased. The desire to operate strict spending limits on Local Government and the Health Service led to bitter in-fighting between the central departments involved and the Treasury, and these conflicts were mirrored in Cabinet between the various Ministers on the one hand and the Chancellor on the other.

At the same time relationships between and within central departments were upset by pressures, from the Prime Minister in particular, to cut the number of civil servants and to shake up the civil service hierarchy.

The White paper of 1982 'Efficiency and Effectiveness in the Civil Service, Government Observations on the Third Report from the Treasury and Civil Service Committee', on all Whitehall departments to publish a detailed breakdown of their costs, responsibilities and staff numbers. The aim was to train a new type of civil service manager and to promote efficiency financial control. It was proposed that the Treasury and Whitechall's Management and personnel Office should co-ordinate the exercise and report progress within several months. However, the white paper rejected the proposals made by many back bench M.P.s that the Comptroller and Auditor General should be able to carry out investigations at their request to ensure more open government and better access to the accounts of all public sector bodies and firms in receipt of private funds.

Nevertheless there is continuing pressure on all civil service department to be more accountable and to introduce efficiency exercises and reduce numbers.

The government announced in 1981 that control of pay and manpower in the civil service was to be transferred from the Civil Service Department (to be abolished) to the Treasury. The importance of this responsibility arises because the government is a major employer , so that the rates of pay and conditions of service that it negotiates have a considerable impact at the level of the economy as a whole.

We also include the Department of the Environment here since it oversees the spending of the local authorities, an important part of total government expenditure.

Departments responsible for micro-economic policy

Several departments are concerned with micro-economic policy i.e. policy relating to particular markets, industries or sectors of the economy.

The Department of Industry is responsible for general industrial policy including overseeing the activities of the National Enterprise Board and government support for research and development, and for the industrial component of regional policy, including financial assistance to industry under the Industry Act. Although major decisions are taken at the Department's headquarters in London, it has a regional net work based on eight regional offices in England. These offices represent the Department in its dealings with industry, local authorities and other organizations.They are also responsible for administering assistance to industry in Assisted Areas. In association with the Scottish Office and Welsh Office, the Department operates a chain of eleven Small Firms Information Centres. As noted in the previous chapter, these centres assist small firms in finding sources of help for financial, legal and technical problems. The department acts as sponsor for various industries, e.g. chemicals, textiles, and is responsible for several nationalized industries, including the British Steel Corporation and the Post Office.

The Department of Trade has four main areas of concern. First, it is responsible for commercial and economic policies that affect the U.K.s international position. It promotes British export and overseas commercial interests, and negotiates on tariffs and other barriers to international trade, Second, it is responsible for competition policy and consumer affairs Third, the Department is the sponsor for the U.K. shipping and civil aviation industries, and is responsible for several nationalized industries.Finally, the Department has general responsibility for the basic legal framework which regulates industrial and commercial enterprises, and administers a number of statutes governing company affairs and insolvency.

The Department of the Environment is responsible, together with the local authorities, for housing policies. The Department of Energy is, of course, concerned with energy policy including the development of North Sea oil and gas. The responsibilities of the Ministry of Agriculture, Fisheries and Food have become more important in recent years on account of the negotiations concerning the E.E.C. Common Agricultural Policy. The Department of Transport is mainly concerned with land transport and in particular for motorways and major trunk roads. Many of the functions previously exercised by the Department were transferred in 1973 to the Manpower Services Commission, which now runs centres and government skill centres and administers government financial assistance for training. But the Department of Employment retains responsibility for policy relating to the trade unions,and relationships between employer and employee.

Departments responsible for social policy

It is not always easy to make a distinction between economic and social policy and some departments are concerned with both. But social policy is the main concern of two departments. The responsibilities of the Department of Health and social Security range from overseeing the operation of the National Health Service to the payment of social security benefits, such as child benefit and retirement pensions. These responsibilities are carried out through an extensive network of regional and local offices.

The Department of Education and Science is concerned with all aspects of education except the universities, which are funded by the provided in conjunction with the local authorities, for whom education is the major item expenditure.

Departments responsible for law, order and external affairs

The Home Office is responsible for maintaining internal law order and the administration of justice. It fulfils these responsibilities via the police, prison, probation, after-care and perhaps surprisingly, the fire service. The external security of the U.K. is in the hands of the Ministry of Defence, which is responsible for all the armed services. Three separate ministries, the War Office, Admiralty and Air Ministry were merged in the early 1970s in an attempt to achieve a more co-ordinated defence policy.

The Foreign and Commonwealth Office is responsible for relationships between the U.K. government and the governments of other countries, i.e. its role is primarily political. But it also engages in activities with an economic content. e.g. providing information and establishing contacts which aid British exporters.

The allocation of responsibilities discussed above is modified in various ways in Scotland, Wales and Northern Ireland. For example, certain regional industrial policy functions in Scotland and Wales are exercised by the Scottish and Welsh offices. Differences in the legal and educational systems of Scotland and England mean that the Scottish Office exercises responsibilities exercised in England by the Home Office and the Department of Education and Science. Internal security in Northern Ireland is the responsibility of the Northern Ireland Office.

The structural structure of central governmnent departments

Differences in responsibilities mean that each department has its own organization and management structure. As we have seen, some departments are highly centralized while others have an extensive network of local offices; some departments operate in one country only, others in numerous countries within the U.K. and overseas.

In a department similar to that shown in Figure political control would be firmly in the hand of the Secretary of state who would be assisted in the day-to-day running of the department by the ministers and parliamentary under-secretaries -all being political appointments. one must not forget however,,the tremendous influence wielded by the fulltime civil servants who generally remain in their jobs, whereas Ministers come and go as their political standing changes.

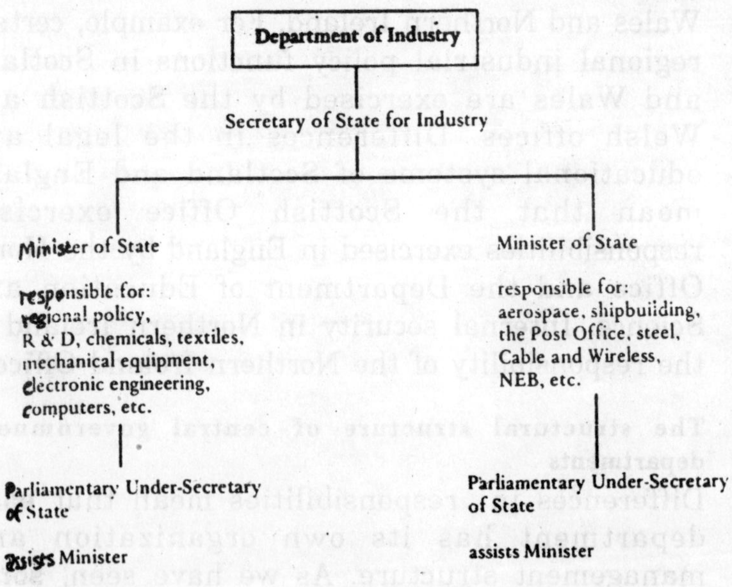

Department of industry.

8 Organisational Power

We make an important distinction between response and action, or reaction as some may prefer to call it. An individual's response is related to his attitudes, feelings and ideas, which we call sentiments. If response is favourable, we can expect positive action. If the response is unfavourable, resistance is a possibility. To act either positively or negatively, the individual must have power in the situation. We must, therefore, examine the nature of power in work organisations.

We find that the notion of power is confused with that of authority. Unfortunately, many believe that the two terms are, interchangeable. We reiterate that authority is the right or capacity to initiate or decide a course of action. Initiation arises from the right to command, one's knowledge, or one's leadership. Power involves the action of implementing or resisting initiations. We can see both positive and negative demonstrations of power. The individual's action completes the cycle of transactions between the order-giver and the order-receiver.

Due to social conventions many think that power is illicit. Black power, student power and union power are all frowned upon by the conservatives; they see authority as the principal social control. The child is punished when he disobeys the directions of his parents; he uses his power to resist. As the child becomes an adolescent and later an adult, his power has to be recognised; he can no longer be effectively punished by spanking.

The argument over power and authority goes on in married life. The actions of one individual may not be in accord with the wishes of another. For example, the wife pleads with her husband for him to cut the lawn, while the husband drinks beer on the patio. The husband goes off to the hotel while the wife asks him not to go. In the circumstances, the actions of the husband may be just as legitimate as the authority of the wife. Authority and power are highly structured in work organisations so that the initiator and the recipient of the initiation are not in the same ambiguous situation as are the husband and wife.

Usually, we find that most people have difficulty in distinguishing between authority and power. They assume that because someone has wide discretion, or occupies a high-status position in the organisation, he necessarily has a great deal of power. He may have it, or he may not. What the reader must learn is to identify the source of power and the direction in which it is being exercise. Then, he is in a position to understand many of the fundamental relationships that exist in his organisation.

What is power?

Power is extremely important in the world of work. Electric power is one of our most important sources of energy. It drives our trains and a great deal of our manufacturing equipment as well as being used for light and heat. Manpower is the oldest source of power. Men laboured without any sophisticated equipment to build such amazing projects as the Pyramids and the Great Wall of China. Manpower is still the source of activity in work organisations, although the brain has largely superseded brawn.

Horsepower is also important in modern operational activities as it is the basis of mechanical activity. Horsepower means the rate of doing work. We classify our motor-cars according to horsepower; the larger the horsepower the more powerful is the car. However, unless we keep the engine in good running condition, the performance of the car is limited to its actual power. Thus, we have two important notions: the capacity of the engine which limits the ultimate power of the car, and its efficiency which determines the car's actual power on the road.

The same type of notions can be applied to an individual's behaviour at work. When an individual acts, he has power. When an individual carries out his task efficiently, he acquires more power than when he carries it out inefficiently. In the same way that a car's power is limited by its engine, the individual's power is limited in the organisation by the nature of his own work role. An individual can acquire greater power only by increasing his efficiency within the limits of his present position, or by expanding the limits of his present position. Basically, the source of an individual's power in a work organisation comes from the performance of his task.

Before we turn to the consideration of factors which determine the source of power of a work role or job, let us consider the two expressions of power. When we press the accelerator hard to the floor, the car surges ahead. We have a positive demonstration of its power. Similarly, when an individual carries out his task he is acting positively; hence, he is demonstrating positive power. An individual can also use his power negatively; for example, he may refuse to carry out an order, or he may carry it out in an incorrect way. By contrast, when a car stops through mechanical failure it simply has no power; we do not say that the car has negative power. Thus, there is a difference between mechanical power, and power as it is found in work organisations.

Negative power may be illustrated by the following example. Suppose we have a central duplicating centre manned by one girl operative. Suppose we approach her and ask her to run off twenty pages of a report we need urgently. Suppose she replies: "Come back tomorrow, I am too busy today". Despite our pleas, she remains adamant that she has no time to do it. Note that she does not say that she will not do the task; she is only delaying it. By doing so, she is exercising negative power. Such a situation is extremely frustrating to the initiator, but he can do little about it. If he can work the equipment, he may use his own power by doing the job himself. This could mean pushing the girl aside but rules, social customs and manners may deter him from such a course of action.

It is interesting to note that negative power is derived from positive power. The refusal to carry out an activity, or to delay it, is an effective demonstration of power only when it holds up the operations of the organisation. If the operations of the organisation are not delayed, then no negative power is exercised. A person can only hold up an operation if he has an important role in it. It follows that those who have considerable positive power can also exercise a great deal of negative power as well. For example, the pilot of a commercial jet can exercise negative power, for without him the plane cannot leave the tarmac.

Many individuals in work organisations are unable to exercise negative power to any great extent. This is due to the fact that they can be easily replaced if they do not carry out the tasks allotted to them. They may be transferred to other jobs, demoted, or even dismissed. If a job requires little skill, a replacement may be easily found. A slack employment market increases this likelihood. However, replacing one person with another may be extremely difficult when there is a shortage of labour, when the job requires special skills, and when the job-holder must be registered or licensed. Thus it is difficult to replace a jet pilot, a surgeon, a boiler attendant or a crane driver.

Distribution of power

We shall consider the horizontal dimension of organisation in this section. Basically, there are three main distributions of power in an organisation. These follow the three basic types of interdependence in the organisation. Interdependence represents the physical organisation of work and power relations are its social expression.

Pooled Power relations: These exist where there is no functional linking between positions, jobs or tasks. Examples include clerks working simultaneously on tasks where no information or processes flow between them; men watching dials or doing ancillary tasks in a semiautomatic or automatic plant; operatives working at fixed stations on a mechanically paced belt; workers individually responsible for the assembly of single units; sales personnel working in separate territories calling on different customers; and individual truck drivers delivering goods to different points. All these individuals work alone; each is responsible for the performance of his own task. No power relationship exists between them because no work flows between them.

Sequential power relations: Here the power is distributed in such a way that the individual performing the preceding work role *always* has power over the person performing the succeeding work role. In a sequential relationship the work is not produced individually as it is in pooled relationship; it is produced by the combined effort of all those working on the process. The individual starting the work in the following situations has the greatest power: the first clerk processing forms or information, the first man of a gang handling goods in loading and unloading situations, the first man processing materials, and the first person commencing an assembly. The critical feature of the sequential power relationship is that a person further down the line cannot complete his task until the person before him has completed his. We can also add that where the person before him does not do his work properly, then, this will affect his particular task. Thus the second person may be dependent on the person before him for the timing of arrival of supplies, work-in-progress, service or tools, and their quantity, quality and cost.

Reciprocal power relations: In this relationship power is distributed according to the importance of the tasks undertaken by the persons occupying two or more work roles. Where there is a skilled maintenance man assisted by an unskilled man, tools and materials are passed from one to another; the two may assist each other in lifting or holding. However, as the performance of the task ultimately depends on the skill of the craftsman, he has greater power because his task is more important than that of the unskilled man. In the operating theatre, the doctor responsible for the anesthetic can cause the death of the patient if he does not do his work properly. The surgeon can literally kill the patient if he makes an error. Which role is the most important? Clearly that of the surgeon, for without him the task of the team cannot be completed successfully. His contribution, and hence his positive power, are greater than those of the other doctor, Power distribution has to be carefully investigated when reciprocal interdependence prevails.

We should note one important effect of technology. Automatic feeds and mechanical conveyor belts have the effect of breaking up sequential power relationships by eliminating human interaction. Pooled power relationships then come into existence with each individual working in isolation. In some cases, reciprocal power relations are broken down into sequential or pooled relationships. Many of the old-fashioned methods of processing involved team work, for example, galvanising rolled steel; these methods are replaced by highly automatic processes. The more highly mechanised or automatic the technology, the more work will be performed by isolated individuals or, in some cases, by isolated pairs.

Power of the subordinate

We have dealt with the distribution of power so far as the horizontal dimension is concerned. What about the vertical dimension? We are so accustomed to think of a subordinate being subject to authority, that we overlook the very real power he has over his superior. The superior may command, order, and instruct, yet the subordinate has the power to carry the task into effect. In fact, the superior is *always* dependent on his subordinate for carrying out allotted tasks. This relationship is fundamental to superior-subordinate relations, even though the degree of power exercised by any individual over his superior may vary considerably.

Let us return to individuals working in pooled relationships. Although each of these has no power relation directly with the others because there are no functional relationships, each individual may wield different degrees of power over his superior. In a production situation the degree of power depends on the quality and quantity of his output; thus, a person producing more than the others has more power over his superior than the others. If the accent is on quality, the individual who produces the higher standard article has greater power than those who produce inferior articles. The salesman who contributes most to the value of sales has the highest degree of power over his superior.

In an educational institution classes are conducted by individual teachers. While the head can evaluate the performance of a teacher he has no control over the teacher's activities; the individual teacher either mars or makes the course. The head may try to take over the teacher's class. If he does, the head reduces his role to that of a teacher. Moreover, because of the pooled power relationship, the superior's condition is limited to his own effort; he cannot influence the behaviour of others in a pooled relationship.

The superior in a sequential power relationship has greater influence over the behaviour of his subordinates in certain simple conditions. Because the work role at the start of the sequential set of tasks has power over succeeding ones, the superior can set the pace or standard of the work by putting himself at the head of the line. He cannot influence the pace of the work by placing himself at the end of the line. However, more complex situations may allow the superior to take over one of the roles of the operatives; he usually has duties that call for detailed scheduling and control. He is, therefore, dependent on his subordinates to carry out their work to the standards specified and according to the timetable laid down.

A working superior can influence the behaviour of the subordinates both through power and through authority where reciprocal power relations apply. The superior wields the greater power by placing himself in the key position. In many situations this needs professional or technical "know-how". The commercial airline captain is a case in point. Where there are a number of small reciprocal groups, such as may exist in a maintenance department, the superior cannot occupy a series of key positions. In this situation he has to content himself with co-ordinating his subordinates by making adjustments between them.

A superior can counter a single individual's power by using his authority. He can reduce the individual's power by transferring him to another work role, or he can destroy it if he dismisses him. However, the superior has to recognise that this method is of limited value as he cannot get rid of all his subordinates as this will destroy his own power base. This is true, quite apart from constraints that may be placed upon him by virtue of policies, conventions and trade union pressures.

We should not be seduced by the argument that the superior has power over his subordinates by the rewards that he can bestow or the penalties that he can apply to his subordinates. There stem from authority and affect the status of an individual and are not acts of power. Moreover, they are applied at particular points of time and, once applied, are exhausted. Yet the power relationship of the sub-ordinate over his superior continues while the tasks go on.

The superior may change the degree of power that a subordinate has over him. This applies particularly to the upper levels of management. By reducing his resource allocations, including establishment and personnel, and capital and operating expenses the superior can cut the power base of a subordinate or alternatively, can increase the power of a subordinate by allocating greater resources to him. Of course, the superior is still dependent on his subordinate for the effective use of the allotted resources; that is, he is still subject to the subordinate's power to carry out his functions and tasks.

We would like to add one final warning.

Although superiors are subject to the power of their subordinates, we should not imagine that the chief executive officer is powerless. On the contrary, he has a great deal of power, particularly over members of the governing body. The chief executive officer is not only responsible for the performance of the entire organization, he controls information that goes to the governing body. He has authority over subordinates and he can manipulate the rewards and penalties available to him; this gives him an impregnable position. There are occasions where particular senior managers are very powerful; in such cases, the chief executive officer has to respect their power. A very effective marketing manager responsible for exceptional sales may be in such a position. Quite clearly, it is in the interests of the chief executive officer to maximise the power of such a manager.

9 A Framework for an Integrated Model

This chapter will display a rather comprehensive schema designed to show the several classes of criteria that may be taken into account in assessing organizational effectiveness. To avoid producing another incoherent laundry list of effectiveness indicators, the schema will attempt to acknowledge the contributions of three distinctive theoretical approaches, and will leave the door open to accommodate the extensions and variations that will certainly arise. The aim is not to produce a neat, unified theory about, or a new definition of, the elusive concept of effectiveness, but rather to produce a frame worn that will aid coherent thought and judicious action by those who are compelled by their leadership roles or their research tasks to choose a definition of effectiveness that suits their unique purposes.

The orientation taken is, in part, sociological. That is it will treat the symbiotic relationships between an organization and its environment of organized and unorganized constituencies. *Constituents* are persons acting in their own interest or as representatives of others and having some form of interdependency with the focal organizational of study. In this inclusive sense, they are "members" of the organization with needs—their own and of others—to be fulfilled.

The orientation taken is, in part, that derived from general systems theory as applied to human organizations. It will be assumed that human organizations share certain universal characteristics of behaving entities, with internally determined capacities and priorities that control their responsiveness to environmental factors.

The orientation is, in part, individualistic and psychological. That is, organizations come into being and are maintained by the activities of persons who are not only members of the organization but simultaneously are persons with attributes and self-identifications that are not derived from nor wholly integrated with their organization. This notion of "partial inclusion" is crucial, for it locates and defines a boundary region of organizations that must be taken into account.

The orientation is, in part, *cybernetic,* by which we mean the analysis of systems for selective use of information in the choice and decision-making activities of organizations to the ends of internal direction and control and of external accommodations.

The orientation is unmistakably practical. For person in constituency roles to choose behaviors that approximate an optimization of those roles, they must continually evaluate the effectiveness of the focal organization and assess its likely future effectiveness. Such evaluations require the selection of effectiveness criteria that are pertinent to the immediate and longer-run interests of the constituency.

This chapter will have three parts. The first will outline a way to merge considerations of effectiveness from three perspectives. The second part will comment on the concept of "integration." The final pages will discuss some properties of advantages and limitations in this approach to the assessment of organizational effectiveness.

Merging conemporary theories

Many people distinguish three main approaches to the understanding of organizational effectiveness. One views an organization as a natural system having its own survival and growth requirements and its own dynamics of activity and change. Another views the organization as a contrived instrument for attainment of specified short-run goals. A third approach treats the organization as an information-processing and decision-making entity, with a focus on factors of organizational control and direction. These are loosely labeled the *natural system model, and goal model,* and the *decision-process model*. We will argue that they are not incompatible and can be treated jointly within a common linking framework.

The approaches are seemingly conflicting in a number of ways. They take different views about the nature and origin of organizational purposes or goals. They take different views of the nature of the relationships between an organization and its environment. They require, for application, measurement of unlike aspect of organizational performances and unlike models for their interpretations.

The natural system model

The core image of an organization in the natural system approach is that of an intact behaving entity, autonomous except for interdependence with a environment in the form of information and energy exchanges. A source of this concept is a general systems theory, which seeks equivalences across an array of behaving systems ranging from the single biological cell to the whole of complex societies. The derivation relevant to formal human work organizations has the name *open systems theory*. The central propositions of this theory are concerned with system boundaries, differentiation and integration of the sub-systems that are "parts" of the focal system, input-transformation-output process, boundary transactions, and system maintenance processes. There exist several good statements and elaborations of this theory, notably those of Baker, Georgopoulos and Cooke, and of Katz and Kahn.

There are a number of variants on these central themes, all illustrative examples are warranted. Georgopoulos has worked out a scheme for assessment and description of work organizations based on the idea that all organizations share a small number of "basic problems" that must be "continuously solved" for the organization to be effective; though these problems relate to work efficiency and output, all of them, such as coordination, and strain control, plainly derive from an image of the organization as a self-maintaining system in dynamic equilibrium within an environment. J.G. Miller regards formal organizations to be fundamentally goalless in the sense that the systemic properties and processes are to be assessed, not narrowly with reference to outputs or end states, but more generally with reference to system equilibrium and maintenance.

There is some empirical support for such a view; for example, a factorial analysis of a roster of effectiveness indicators gave factors that were, in the main, interpretable as system maintenance and adaptivity factors rather than goal achievement factors. Other variants on the natural system model incorporated the goal model in the sense that the focus is on optimizing system-environment relationships: "effectiveness" implies the output of goods or services to the environment of kinds and amounts that assure continuing and adequate inputs to the system.

The natural system model forces attention to certain aspects of organizational effectiveness that, until recently, were largely overlooked or undervalued:

1. The model suggests that effectiveness should be described and evaluated with reference to all attributes of the system that have some significant function in its adaptation, maintenance, and transformation processes.

2. There is a strong implication that effectiveness indicators must be treated as *intact sets*,, not as indicators to be inherently and independently valued.
3. The model allows the idea that the meaning of a given indicator may be contingent in the sense that it may have different, or even opposite, value implications in different contexts.
4. Finally, the model moderates the distinction between "outcome" variables, on the one hand, and "causal" variables, on the other for there is operating a network of linkages that may be causal in both directions.

These features of the natural system model are suggestive rather than definitive as to the practical measurement of organizational effectiveness. It is not feasible to measure *all* attributes of an organization; selection of relevant aspects is an empirical matter to be guided by general systems theory and prior organizational research. *Inact sets* of indicators are needed to accommodate the contingencies and interactions that are known to operate with force; the "intact set" can, at best, be a simplified representation of the complex reality. The "outcomes" of interest are to defined by a linear model, but are themselves system characteristics such as stability, growth, decline, and change.

The goal model

The goal model employs the clear assumption that there are definable purposes or goals, such that the effectiveness of an organization can be represented by the attainment of, or progress toward, these goals. Additional criteria may be invoked when there are instrumental goals or states necessary for attainment of main goals.

As in the case of the natural system model, several variants exist. The most prominent of these variants is that specifying economic goals defined by the owner. Other variants emphasize emergent institutionalized goals sustained by the values of diverse constituencies and somewhat insulated from the purposes of the current leaders.

The goal approach views an organization as an entity contrived and controlled to serve the purposes of the key influential, including owners, managers, and others, whether "inside" the organization, who have some controlling power in defining the operative purposes of the organization. The purposes, of course, need not be selfishly individualistic, but may be altruistic, public spirited, expressive of societal norms, or goals chosen by consensus or compromise among members and other constituencies.

The goal model has utility. It directs attention to the seeming purposefulness of some organizations. It forces attention to the value perspectives and assumptions that lead to the dominance of some goals over others. It makes explicit the linkage of the organization to its value-laden environment. It provides a convenient analytic tool for mapping the causal relationships between antecedent conditions, instrumental goals and means, and the ultimate or highest priority goals—a property of high importance in the context of policy formation, decision making, and action.

It is currently fashionable to be critical of the goal model, on grounds that it does not fit well some observed characteristics of organizations. Goals appear to change in priority rather too easily; goal sets are often internally incompatible; organizational behavior often contradicts espoused goals; organizations often survive indefinitely or grow without even realizing any of their espoused goals; it is often difficult or impossible to get responsible spokesmen to agree on the nature of an organization's goals; organizations often are observed to act first and then discover later a "goal" to justify what has happened.

These problems are put in perspective if one assumes, as we propose to do, that the goal model refers not to some goals that are inherent in the organizational system itself, but instead to goals of persons related in some way to the organization, Purposiveness and goal formation are thus to be regarded as *psychological* phenomena, external to the organization but forming a crucial aspect of its environment. When managers, owners or other influential groups or categories of people form their goals *for* an organization, these goals can become operative to the extent that they impinge on the organization's processes for environmental exchange, accommodation, and self-maintenance. The goal model makes eminently good sense when viewed as a model for describing the purposive forces exerted on the organizational system; it makes little or no sense when viewed as a model for self-generated purposiveness within organization systems.

In short, we propose to put "goals" on the other side of the organization versus environment dichotomy.

Some will think that the foregoing ideas are not consequential for understanding organizational effectiveness. For some applications in analysis or evaluation that is true, for the distinction becomes trivial when there is consensus among all influential goal sources—a condition likely to be found only in very small or very autonomous organizations where the person of an influential is indistinguishable from his or her organizational role and function.

The decision-process model

The core image underlying the decision-process model arises from the notion that organizations develop distinctive ways for employing information resources in the service of systemic integrity and goal attainment. These ways of dealing with information can be observed and measured; they can be assessed against criteria of intrinsic merit established by the logic of information usage; they can be assessed against "external" criteria of organizational outcomes or states in the domains of systemic integrity and goal attainment. In this context, an effective organization is one that optimizes the processes for getting, storing, retrieving, allocating, manipulating, interpreting, and discarding information. The effective organization is capable of accommodating a wide range of kinds of information. The effective organization has physical and human facilities capable of monitoring the quality of information and capable of the selective employment of information in problem-solving and behavior-controlling activity.

A number of people concerned about organizational effectiveness have focused on information-management and decision-making processes, and have done so from widely disparate disciplinary orientations. We will not attempt a census of contributions, but will give a few examples to illustrate the variety.

Jerald Hage is one of several who have offered cybernetic theories of organizational effectiveness. His book treats communication channels and networks, feedback loops, selective mobilization of information for specific uses, and the like; his treatment is highly evaluative, with reference to goal priorities, conflict resolution, forward planning, and system maintenance. His references to systemic integrity and goal attainment are explicit.

Other representing a behavioral approach to organizational decision processes include March and Simon on search behavior, limited rationality; Pattigrew on the political and power aspects of strategic decisions; Likert on participative, group-based decision processes. Argyris and Schon put the matter into a framework of organizational learning, in which they link individual-level choice processes to organizational norms and processes for information management. Many others could be named. What they have in common is the view that organizations are, among other things, information-processing and decision-making entities that can be, and commonly are, evaluated against (a) rational standards of intrinsic goodness of decisions made; appropriateness of decision process; or impact on systemic integrity or goal attainment.

Collateral to the behavioral approaches to the effectiveness of organizational decision processes are those approaches focusing primarily on the "behavior" of data, not the behavior of persons. It is fair for the assessor of organizational effectiveness to note the extent and appropriateness of the use of mechanical, electronic, and statistical—mathematical decision aids. More, however, is not necessarily better.

Certain features of the decision process models of organizational effectiveness deserve note. They tend to emphasize dynamic processes over time. They tend to be oriented to further effectiveness rather than to the recent past, compared with the goal attainment indicators that tend to be historical, and the systemic integrity process models that tend to emphasize change, adaptivity, and response to environmental intrusions. These complementary dimensions of the three models are highly significant, for their inclusion in an integrated model allows estimation of organizational effectiveness over a future span of time under changing external conditions.

The issue of fit of decision processes to the organizations' situation is crucial and difficult, requiring differentiation among organizations as to their youth or maturity, whether in information-rich or information-poor environments, whether possessing a relatively stable or instable goal structure, whether embedded in a simple or a complex array of influential constituencies.

It is evident that the decision-process model confronts the assessor of organizational effectiveness with a very large and diverse array of concepts and specific variables for measurement and evaluation. However, this is likewise true for the natural system and goal models. All three are amenable to simplifying hierarchical organization of concepts and to the devising of feasible operations for their measurement.

An integration of models

There is no need to choose one among the goal, natural system, and decision-process models, rejecting the others, for they are not competitive as explanatory devices; instead, they are nicely complementary, referring to different but interdependent facets of organizational behavior. As aids in understanding organizational effectiveness they differ in scope and utility. The natural system model appears, from a researcher's perspective, the more comprehensive as it offers strong advantages as to ultimate convergence with related theories growing out of other disciplines. Indeed, some theorists would attempt to force goal attainment and decision making into the mold of the natural system model, even though such a merging (compared with joint usage) would raise difficult and perhaps unsolvable problems as to organizational identity and boundary. The suggested central role of the natural system model does not preclude the use and testing of propositions arising from the other models. The "integration" of the three is to be facilitated by restricting the goal model to treatments of the goals imposed on the organization by persons acting in roles that are not integral to the focal organization; by restricting the decision-process model to its own limited domain.

One may well ask what sort of an "integration" is proposed. It may seem to consist only of accepting all popular ideas and fitting them together in a patchwork design. When Pennings and Goodman took this route, colleagues scolded them gently for doing so, but it may well be that the design need not be merely a patchwork. The "integration" may take at least two forms of interest and utility.

Triangulation

Drawing on a little optimism, and some confidence in the orderliness of Mother Nature, one can assert that for most organizations. Most of the time, there must be a state of compatibility among the three domains of effectiveness that have been described. Systemic integrity must exist in sufficient degree of balance among the component factors; goals must be attained to some sufficient degree—particularly those describable as system outputs of kinds that sustain resource input transactions; decision and control processes must be sufficiently appropriate and workable to deal with the problems relating to goal structures, systemic maintenance, and the maintenance of a sufficiently efficient goal-oriented input-throughput-output system. Insufficiency in any one of these areas, or even a single subpart of any one, puts the organization at risk. Sufficiency, in each case, is to be defined with reference to the impact of each domain of effectiveness on the other two. Assessment in all three domains, with cross references, should provide some relief from the prevailing criticisms of both theorists and practitioners—that the natural system model does not say enough about goal attainment, that the goal model ignores significant organizational properties of predictive, diagnostic, and corrective importance, and that the decision-process model has rather little topical content of a generalizable sort useful for assessing trends and making comparisons among organizations.

Multiple integrations

The term *effectiveness* is evaluative by definition and implies that some coherent set of interests and value preferences is brought to bear. An important contribution of open system theory has been the growing awareness of a need to take into account different value perspectives. These are of at least four general classes:

1. Perspectives arising from the interests of subordinate and superordinate organizational units, in large hierarchical organizations
2. Perspectives arising from interests of members of the organization who import personal values and purposes that can, at best, be only partially reflected within the focal organization
3. Perspectives arising from interests of "outside" persons or organizations of interdependence
4. Perspectives representing the general societal or public interest.

This is a formal way of saying that organizational effectiveness can, and indeed must, be evaluated from the perspectives of different interested parties such as people in higher echelons in the case of hierarchically linked organizations, members of the organization, exchange partners, and the general public.

Organizations, as such, have no value perspective of "their own" even though they may take on properties compatible with some distinctive value priorities. The multiple value perspectives all arise outside of the organization, even though they may, in the case of members, be modified by the individual's experiences as member. They are legitimated as factors in the assessment of organizational effectiveness to the extent that they are linked with persons or sets of co-acting persons having some power to establish or modify constraints on what the focal organization may do or try to do. The concept of "constituencies" thus takes on prime importance. The treatment of constituencies by Pennings and Goodman is illuminating in this context.

Constituents, then, as actors on the scene, are the principle "integrators." They integrate in unique ways, according to their respective value orientations and transaction relationships to the focal organization, and within the limits of their information and analytic resources. The act of integration consists merely of attending simultaneously to those interest, and forming judgments as a basis for actions. Constituents are persons, although they may act and react as representatives of unorganized but likeminded constituents. Some constituencies—say dispersed product customers—may attend only to product availability, utility, and cost; others, such as employees, managers, or owners, will work with a richer array of effectiveness indicators, different sets of values, and with greater potential for imposing their goal preferences on the organization. This is, of course, a rather untidy conception of how organizational effectiveness is assessed by the pertinent actors, but if that is the way the world operates we must accept it.

There are two significant observations to be derived from the foregoing assertions. First, we must abandon the notion that there exists some "true" or "objective" degree of organizational effectiveness for a given focal organization; the effectiveness estimates are always plural—potentially different and equally valid estimates for each constituent or constituency population. Second, there are powerful social dynamics operating that have the effect of inducing some degree of compatibility in value perspectives among key constituencies; for example, constituencies holding value perspectives distinctively unlike those of key constituencies, and lacing means for imposing their own values, tend to change their values or cease to be a significant constituency; that is, they die or quit or take their trade elsewhere. Third, it is important for the observer or researcher to identify the constituency or constituencies for whom effectiveness is being evaluated.

The researcher or theoretician is in a privileged position, as the value perspective applied may be one's own or someone else's. If one's own, the integration involves equal consideration of all three of the effectiveness domains I have described.

Members as constituents

The schema that has been outlined clearly places members of an organization in roles as constituents, not as integral components of the organization itself. As constituents, members are differentiated from other constituents only by the comparative immediacy of their power to influence the organization and by their direct and value-laden concern with all three domains of organizational effectiveness. Like other constituents, they integrate evaluative information with reference to their own value perspectives, but commonly do so as members of organized constituency sets, or as representatives of unorganized but like-minded constituency sets. From the research perspective, the member-constituents are of unparalled importance and utility, as they are readily observable in their behavior as constituents while acting in their organizational role and sittings and, in addition, are qualified informants about other constituencies.

10 The Importance of Leadership and Organisation Management

Leadership and management communication affect nearly all aspects of organizational life. Leaders help guide individuals, groups, and entire organizations in establishing goals and sustaining action to support goals. Managers fulfill specific organizationally assigned roles designed to direct and evaluate the work of others. Managers are expected to be leaders, although not all managers exhibit leadership behaviors. In fact, leadership communication can come from virtually anyone in the organization, with the effectiveness of leadership and management communication directly relating to organizational success and work satisfaction.

But what exactly do we mean by leadership and management communication? There are literally hundreds of definitions of what leaders do and what is considered to be leadership. Chances are our personal definition of leadership may vary from that of our friends and may even change from situation to situation. We might call an individual a leader, for example, because of the person's election to the presidency of a particular organization. At another time we might say that the same individual is not a leader because he or she does not exhibit leadership behaviors expected from the president. In other words, we expected leadership from the legitimate position of the presidency, but when the president does not exhibit leadership behaviors, we say the president is not a leader.

Leadership takes place through communication. Leaders communicate about needed change, translate intentions into reality, propose new strategies, and help sustain action to support decisions. Leadership communication is a process of influence whereby leaders attempt to convince followers to attain specific goals or broad organizational outcomes. The ability to influence is based on the leader's position, credibility to a follower group, analysis and technical skills, and overall communication competence. People can be assigned the position of leader; however, leadership occurs not from the assignment itself but through communication behaviors in interactions with others.

Management fulfills specifically defined roles designed to facilitate work to support organizational goals. Managers are given legitimate power to influence the behavior of subordinates. They are charged with obtaining routine compliance with the operating procedures and expectations of the organization. It is hoped, of course, that managers can exceed routine compliance and instill in subordinates a desire for excellence that goes beyond merely acceptable performance. Whether resulting in routine compliance or a desire for excellence, managerial influence occurs through human communication. Based on the formal superior-subordinate relationships, managerial communication is directed to work assignments, work evaluation, needed changes, and all other aspects of directing organizational action for goal achievement.

Both leadership and management communication are powerful organizational influences. Communication relationships between managers and subordinates influences innovation, decision making, work satisfaction, and perceptions of organizational climate. Leadership communication, whether exhibited by managers or other influential organizational members, becomes the vision of the organization that directs and redirects all organizational activity. As Warren Bennis and Burt Nanus suggest, "effective leadership can move organizations from current to future states, create visions of potential opportunities for organizations, instill within employees commitment to change, and instill new cultures and strategies in organizations that mobilize and focus energy and resources."

Leadership and management communication is part of the sense-making activities of the organization. It helps members develop priorities and determine what is needed by the organization. It influences decision making, transmits communication rules, and contributes to the shared realities that become the organization's culture. As such, leadership and management communication charts the course of action for the organization. The effectiveness of this communication, therefore, is central to organizational excellence.

Theories of leadership and management

Thousands of articles have been written about leadership and management. We talk about the need for leadership in our communities, in the organizations in which we work, and in government. Yet trying to describe how leadership and management work and how they should work remains a difficult and often controversial task. Are leaders born with leadership talents? What styles do successful leaders employ? Are some people simply in the right time and place to assume leadership responsibility? What type of leader is John Mitchell? What type of manager? Is there a difference? What can we do it increase our leadership effectiveness?

Theories of leadership and management describe leaders and managers in terms of personal traits or characteristics, preferences for leadership styles or approaches, and responsiveness to leadership requirements in specific situations. Before were explore trait, style, and situational theories of leadership, please complete the leadership experience exercise. The exercise will give you a profile of some of your attitudes and experiences with leadership that you can compare with major theories of leadership and management.

You now have before you an assessment of your personal theory of leadership. As you begin to evaluate major theories of leadership and management think about your own personal theory and what is needed for leadership effectiveness.

Trait approaches

Early theories of effective leadership assumed that leaders had innate traits that made them effective. That is, great leaders were considered to be born with the ability for leadership. This theory of the "great man" first surfaced in th writings of the early Greeks and Romans and is prevalent today among those who believe that leadership cannot be developed-that you either have leadership qualities or not.

Over eighty years of research has attempted to define traits or personality characteristics that best predict the effective leader. Lists of desirable traits have numbered approximately eighty characteristics, but the trait approach has failed to define clearly a stable set of characteristics associated with effective leadership. Even the concept of what is effective remains open to question.

Ronald Applbaum, Edward Bodaken, Kenneth Sereno, and Karl Anatol suggest that effective leaders are higher in intelligence than other group members, are able to adapt to changing situations, and are wiling to deviate more than other group members from traditions and norms, all contributing to the perception of others that the individual is a leader. These researchers suggest that "perhaps leadership is not so much a function of deviancy as it is a function of knowing how much and when to deviate."

Applbaum and his colleagues' observations reflect the findings of Ralph Stogdill and Alvin Coons, which suggest that leaders more than others are higher in intelligence, scholarship, responsibility, participation, and socioeconomic status. Keith Daavis suggests that intelligence, social maturity initiative, and human relations abilities affect leadership. He does caution, however, that we really do not understand cause-and-effect relationships between traits and effective leadership.

When we study group leaders who emerge on their own rather than being appointed or elected, we find relatively low communication apprehension and a willingness to participate verbally in group activities. Those not emerging as leaders are more likely to exhibit communication behaviors that include rigidity, authoritarian statements, and generally offensive verbalizations.

Despite the importance of intelligence, communication ability, and situational adaption, the approach of identifying traits has generally failed to explain effective leadership. This approach simply does not provide a comprehensive explanation of how leaders intact with followers and meet the needs of specific circumstances.

To illustrate the difficulty of establishing a trait approach for leadership, identify two leaders you would characterize as effective. Describe their personality traits and characteristics in relation to the groups they lead. Now identify two leaders whose effectiveness you question. What traits and characteristics do thy exhibit? Do your effective and ineffective leaders share similar characteristics? How do they differ? What leadership traits do you exhibit? How effective are theso characteristics?

Style approaches

The style approach also applies to understanding leadership and management communication. As Wayne Pace has suggested, "managerial style is, however, quite directly related to three elements over which a manager has some control: (1) a manager's assumptions about people and what motivates them; (2) a manager's perceptions of what he or she can do to influence others; and (3) a manager's views of the resources over which he or she has control."

Style theories for understanding leadership attempt to identify a range of general approaches leaders use to influence goal achievement. These approaches are theorized to be based on the leader's assumptions about what motivates people to accomplish goals. Particular approaches also ar thought to reflect complex relationships among the personal characteristics of th leader the requirements of the situation at hand, and the resources over which the leader and followers have control or influence.

Chief among the style theories is the autocratic-to-democratic continuum first proposed by Ralph White and Ronald Lippit. This continuum suggests that leadership can be understood as ranging in behavior from autocratic to democratic. The three primary styles identified are autocratic, democratic, and laissez-faire.

The atuocratic leader or manager makes decisions with little influence from others. Thus leaders rolle others what to do and usually enforces sanctions against those who choose not to comply. the autocratic leader views followers as essential for goal achievement but usually feels little responsibility for subordinate needs and relationships. Some research suggests that autocratically led groups produce more in quantity than democratically led groups but that th quality of output is better when more democracy is practiced.

All of us have been involved autocratic leaders. Can you identify a successful autocratic leader and one who is not so successful? What makes the difference? Is there a best time for autocratic management? What do you lose in the process of being an autocrat?

Democratic leaders involve followers in decision making. They assume creativity will be greater and there will be more broad-based support for goals if participation is high. Democratic leaders assume followers are able to participate in decision making. These leaders, therefore, attempt to generate a climate in which problem solving can take place while interpersonal relationships are preserved.

Democratic leaders, as do autocrats, both

succeed and fail. Now identify a successful democratic leader and one who is not so successful. As you did for the autocrats, attempt to determine the difference. What made the approach work for one and not the other? From your personal leadership profile, attempt to place your theory on the autocratic-to-democratic continuum.

The *laissez-faire* leader is really and example of a nonleader. This leader expects individuals and groups to make their own decisions. The laissez-faire leader takes a "hands off" approach and contributes information only when asked by group members. This leader how little direct concern for individuals or goals. Groups can succeed with laissez-faire leaders. Their success depends greatly, however, on the abilities of the group and the willingness to work with little or no leadership. Have you ever been in a group with laissez-faire leadership? What happened? How did you feel about that type of working experience?

Robert Tannenbaum and Warren Schmidt have expanded the concept of the autocratic-to-democratic continuum by describing it in terms of the use of authority by the leader and the area of freedom for subordinates. As you can see, the autocratic end of the continuum is characterized by the manager using authority to make and announce decisions with little decision-making input from subordinates. As the approach to leading becomes more democratic, more input from subordinates is asked for and utilized.

How would you describe John Mitchell on this

continuum? What are his basic assumptions about people? How are those assumptions reflected?

Perhaps the best known of the style theories for leadership and management is the one proposed in 1964 and updated through 1985 by Robert Blake and lane Mouton. The Blake and Mouton Managerial Grid suggests that leadership styles or approaches are based on two central dimensions; concern for relationships with people and concern for task production. The balances leaders and managers make between these dimensions have become known as the leadership styles of impoverished, middle-of-the-road, country club, task and team management.

Impoverished management. Impoverished management is characterized by low concern for interpersonal relationships and task accomplishment. The impoverished leader makes few attempts to influence people toward task or goal achievement. His leader frequently dislikes leadership responsibilities and lets others take responsibility that rightfully belongs to the leader. This leader often is uncomfortable with leadership and intellectually resists the need for it. many impoverished leaders are excellent technically; they have been promoted to supervision or management because of strong technical skills. Technical skill, however, do not prepare them for managing people or letting others accomplish tasks that the leaders themselves have been used to doing. Impoverished leaders may even think that if people would "do their jobs" there would be little real need for leadership. Such leaders are most often found in legitimate or formal leadership positions rather than in emergent positions as the choice of a group of peers. These leaders may be primarily responsible for the failure of a group of peers. These leaders may be primarily responsible for the failure of a group, yet they can rarely claim much credit for a group's success. Groups with impoverished leaders often succeed despite the leader and through the emergent leadership of other group members.

Middle-of-the-road management. Middle-of-the-road management balances task and people concerns. Sometimes referred to as *compromise* leadership, the middle-of-the-road leader negotiates and compromises in order to achieve workable agreements and directions for action. This leader is more concerned with practical versus excellent solutions. The middle-of-the-road leader will seek the "middle" position to maintain a group where everyone has some stake in the decision. The compromise positions of middle-of-the-road leaders have been criticized a Band-aids on the wounds of more serious problems. Critics suggest that middle-of-the-road leadership provides short-term solutions guaranteeing long-term problems. Middle-of-the-road leaders frequently are found in middle management, where compromise between the needs of subordinates and top management seems inevitable. In fact, the difficult position of middle management has often been referred to as the sandwich position because of the pressures from below and from above—pressures that often result in the need for compromise.

Country club management. The country club leader wants to be liked and to have a group of followers who feel supported by the leader. This leader provides an interpersonal relationship bond that is low on task emphasis and high in interpersonal support. country club leaders may want the task accomplished but will not take steps to emphasize this element to others if group members are to highly task oriented. Country club managers are frequently observed doing the work of their subordinates rather than insisting that their subordinates exhibit high standards of performance. These managers may not develop the abilities of their subordinates. However, they may lead successful groups when group members themselves have high task motivation and only require interpersonal support to maintain motivation.

Task. Often referred to as autocratic leadership, the task management leader is concerned with goals or task achievement and exhibits little concern for personal relationships. This leader makes decisions and expects compliance. He or she often enforces decisions with little subordinate input and is willing to defend his or her position when necessary. Task leaders often exhibit win-lose conflict style preferences. the task leader values efficiency and will make quick and timely decisions. Task leadership, as do other approaches, requires having appropriate information in which to make good decisions; but by showing low concern for people, such leaders may alienate others to the point that they withhold information that might improve decision making. Task leadership, however, may be appropriate when a group is hopelessly deadlocked on an issue and someone needs to take responsibility for making a decision. Furthermore, surveys of top management in leading American companies indicate that task leadership is a prevalont style preference among highly influential managers.

Team management. Exhibiting high concern for both task and interpersonal relationships, team leaders emphasize goal accomplishment while supporting people. Team leadership fosters a sense of "we" with high performance standards. This leadership shares decision making and strives for problem solving designed to solve rather than postpone problems. Team leaders respect differing points of view and value diversity as long as all contribute to the group effort. Team leaders, however, must have capable and willing team members for successful efforts. Although the style is highly desirable, team leaders depend on team followers for their style of leadership to work. Team members who support each other but who do not have enough ability or information to work on problems will not be able to produce a high-quality decision. In other words, willingness to be a tam member does not ensure a solid team, and team leadership only produces excellent results with a capable team.

To better understand the styles approach to leadership, identify a series of leaders with whom you have had contact and who exhibited each of these five approaches. Try to determine how you reacted to each and how effective his or her leadership was. From your own experiences, what determines whether a particular style is effective or ineffective?

Situational approaches

Both the trait and style approaches failed to describe comprehensively why particular approaches would in one set of circumstance s and tail in another. In response to this difficulty, situational, or contingency, approaches were developed to understand better how leaders interact with followers and the requirements of a particular environment.

In 1967, Fred Fiedler pioneered understanding leadership styles based on the concept of *contingencies*. He suggested that leader effectiveness could be evaluated only in relationship to how style choices related to contingencies in particular situations. Task and interpersonal relationships were important, but also to be considered were the leader's power position and how rewards and punishment were handled. Sometimes powerful leaders had good follower relationships to accomplish well-defined tasks a favorable condition for leadership. At other ties the leader's power position was in question, with an ambiguous goal to accomplish. In the latter circumstance, leader-member relationships could become strained, generating an overall unfavorable condition. According to fielder the approach or style an effective leader chose depended on a combination of task, relationship, power, and situational contingencies.

Building on the work of Robert Black and Jane Mouton, paul Hersey and Kenneth Blanchard proposed a concept of leadership that suggested that the appropriateness and effectiveness of leadership behaviors could not be determined by the specific behavior of the leader but by the appropriateness of the behavior in a particular situation. hersey and Blanchard's Situational Leadership theory postulated that effectiveness of a particular leader was related to the leader's selection of behavior apporpriate to the maturity level of the follower group. Maturity was based on achievement-motivation, ability, education, experience, and the willingness to participate responsibly in goal-oriented activity. In other words, the maturity level of the follower group was the primary factor that determined an effective leadership style. Hersey and Blanchard described situational leadership as dependent on concern for relationships, concern, for task, and concern for maturity of followers. They saw four general styles of situational leadership; telling, selling, participating, and delegating.

The selling style also has high task emphasis, but it has a higher relationship emphasis than the telling style. The selling style is characterized by the leader's attempt to convince followers of the importance of the goal and the leader's definition of how the goal is to be accomplished. The selling style is appropriate for a follower group mature enough to accept some responsibility for decisions and actions.

Unlike the team style of Blake and Mouton, the participating style has high relationship and low task emphases in order to stimulate the creativity of a matur group of followers. The leader supports relationships and encourages participation in decision making because followers and sufficiently mature to contribute to good decisions and support decisions with appropriate action.

The final style, delegating, has low task and low relationship emphases based on high follower maturity. In other words, the leaders lets followers take responsibility for decisions and actions based on a maturity level sufficient for that responsibility. The leader actually passes leadership to the group in the delegating style.

Based on the Hersey and Blanchard description of effective leadership, a mature follower group with considerable experience in a particular set of circumstances may become an immature group when faced with new challenges. An effective leader, therefore, would be required to delegate under the first circumstance and possibly return to the telling style when circumstances change.

As an example of how situational leadership might be applied, consider the case of an advertising account team in transition from one account to another. The creative group-artists, writers, and producers-was very familiar with the products manufactured by their former client. They knew how the products worked, what their advantages were over major competitors, and how to produce budget-effective commercials the client liked. When the client was sold to a major competitors, the needs, of the situation changed. The entire creative team was transferred to the new owner's account with only limited responsibility to their old product line. In fact, the assignment was to integrate the old product line with the new owner's products. Quality advantages, pricing structure, client tastes, and budgets all were changed. The talent of the creative staff remained the same, but the changing assignment contributed to less "maturity" in the group. The account executive supervisor could no longer use a delegating style under dramatically changed circumstances. Although not reverting to the extreme of the telling style, the group's supervisor used a selling style in order to bring about quickly needed changes without losing the account to other agencies. The fact that the account stayed with the same creative team despite a change in client ownership attested to the flexibility of the manager and the appropriate application of a leadership style reflecting changing business needs. Leadership effectiveness, from the situational perspective, can be described as style selection appropriate to the needs of followers in a particular circumstance. With this approach, situational analysis becomes as important as task and relationship behavior.

We have described trait, style, and situational approaches to understanding leadership and management communication. By now you have probably recognized that these approaches are complementary, each building on the other. In other words, our approaches for studying leadership occurs. We look at the traits, styles, and the circumstances in which a particular leader influences his or her group. We use our traits, style, and situational approaches together to help us explain why a particular leadership effort was successful or how the effort might have been more effective. We are not trait, style, or situational leaders but leaders who exhibit traits, styles, and reactions to specific situations. The approaches we have just studied should help us evaluate our own efforts and better understand the efforts of others.

Throughout our discussion we have described leadership as responsibility of managers, as well as an influence process that engages those other than managers. We will now describe important distinctions between leadership and management communication. Keep in mind, however, that whereas managers need to be leaders, excellent organizations, require leadership from all organizational positions.

Distinctions between leadership and management

Waren Bennis and burt Nanus make important distinctions between leaders and managers when they suggest that

> the problem with many organizations, and especially the ones that are failing, is that they tend to be overmanaged and underled. They may excel in the ability to handle the daily routine, yet never question whether the routine should be done at all. There is a profound difference between management and leadership, and both are important. "To manage" means "to bring about to accomplish, to have change of our responsibility for, to conduct." "Leading" is "influencing, guiding in direction, course, action, opinion." The distinction is crucial. managers are people who do things right and leaders are people who do the right thing. The difference may be summarized as activities of vision and judgment-effectiveness versus activities of mastering routines-efficiency.

Bennis and Nanus further contend that the vision leaders provide is the clearest of all distinctions between leaders and managers. To provide vision requires marshalling the "spiritual and emotional" resources of the organization as reflected in its values, commitment, and aspirations. Management, on the other hand, is charged with directing the physical resources of the organization, its people, machines, and products. Competent managers can get work done efficiently, but excellence comes from leaders who inspire followers to emotional involvement with work and their organization. Bennis and Nanus state, "Great leaders often inspire their followers to high levels of achievement by showing them how their work contributes to worthwhile ends. It is an emotional appeal to some of the most fundamental human needs-the need to be important, to make a difference, to feel useful, to be a part of a successful and worth while enterprise."

The increasing complexity of an information society places new demands on leaders and managers. The sheer volume of information available for organizational decision making complicates the development of organizational vision and the direction of organizational activities. This volume of information, when coupled with fast-paced technological changes, puts a new emphasis on the need for leadership from diverse organizational positions. In a complicated information society, the development of vision and the generation of emotional commitment to the work and values of an organization can no longer rest solely with leaders at the top of the organization or with the management team that directs organizational activity.

Put simply, the information society requires leadership from diverse organizational positions. Managers will continue to fulfill specific organizational roles for the direction of work. It is hoped that those in the role of manager will also provide leadership and generate commitment to the values of the organization. However, the management role represents the formal organizational hierarchy and, as such, is deeply involved in efficiently planning and implementing what the organization has decided to do. Put another way, managers are responsible for generating enough stability for efficient work to be accomplished. Leaders, on the other hand,are responsible for generating enough change continually to adapt to new circumstances. Thus, the competencies for effective leaders and managers are not the same. Complex organizations need leadership exhibited by those who identify emerging problems and opportunities, whether they fulfill the role of manager or not.

We can readily understand how a manager becomes a leader when inspiring subordinates to excellent performance. What we do not as readily see is the leadership role of the subordinate who identifies a needed work change, a possible new product, or an improved service opportunity and proceeds to influence others to share that vision of an improved organization. This subordinate's assumption of leadership responsibility is highly desirable for th fast paced information age.

Determinants leadership effectiveness

Thus far we have discussed whether leaders are born or can be developed, what traits are associated with effective leadership, how leadership styles relate to the maturity of followers and to particular leadership situations, and how leadership contributes to establishing organizational vision. Throughout our discussion we have contended that both leadership and management are enacted through human communication. With this perspective, we will now examine how communication competencies, influence, and analysis abilities contribute to leadership effectiveness.

Communication competencies as determinants of leadership effectiveness

A recurring theme throughout this competence is necessary for organization excellence. Knowledge, sensitivity, skills, and values all must be understood and developed for both individuals and entire organizations to be effective in our emerging information era. Nowhere is communication competency more important than when individuals are attempting to lead and established vision and direction for organizations.

Research on managerial effectiveness and perceptions of effectiveness supports the importance of communication competence. In the famous works of Chris Argyris, Peter Drucker, and Warren Bennis and Burt Nanus, communication effectiveness is described as a central element for overall managerial effectiveness. communication encoding, decoding, and interaction capabilities are described as factors necessary for communication and overall managerial competence.

Predispositions for leadership communication

As we have previously discussed, the knowledge, sensitivity, skills, and values we bring to particular situations powerfully influence our behavior choices. Whether or not we choose to attempt leadership is related to our assessment of our own competencies, the needs of the situation, the receptivity of a following group, and our potential ability to influence.

Those high anxiety about communication, "for example, are less likely to engage in leadership attempts than those lower in communication apprehension. Highly task-oriented individuals are more preferring close interpersonal relationships are more likely to adopt style reflecting their concern for people. Although the grids in these figures represent behavioral approaches used for leadership and management, they can also be understood as preferences individuals bring to leadership and managerial situations. Concern for task and people relationships, when coupled with an assessment of follower maturity, influences behavior choices in specific circumstances. But concerns for task and people relationships, follower maturity, personal assessments of communication competence, and assessments of influence or power positions are also reflected in our predispositions for leadership communication-predispositions that subsequently influence strategies objectives and tactical choices.

Strategic communication objective for leadership

We described strategic objectives for conflict as the general game plans for conducting communication based on preferences or predispositions for conflict and on assessments of the probable outcomes within particular contexts. Communication strategies for leadership can be described in the same way. Tactics, then, ae the specific behavior choices made by leaders to influence followers in specific situations and to support overall strategies.

Autocratic strategies are used by leaders who seek to have followers implement decisions with little or no follower input. John Mitchell can decide that the current complaints at invest Corporation call for autocratic strategies. He can announce that he will continue to determine when decisions will be made and that his technical decision will not be subject to question. He can choose to ignore complaints that he is "invisible" and continue to view leadership as a technical contribution. These autocratic strategies are possible as long as top management supports him.

John also has choices among more participative strategies. He can encourage senior lab members to suggest ways in which he can work with them in a team atmosphere. He can compromise about the number of details he will handle personally and the amount of time he is taking to make decisions. He can seek to establish more open and supportive relationships in order to become a more "visible" manger. Finally , John can use avoidance or laissez-fair strategies and ignore the complaints he is hearing. He has the avoidance obtain because of his legitimate power position al laboratory manager. He can ignore much of the discontent as long as he retains the support of senior management.

John's selection of strategies is related to his

assessment of what is needed for leadership and his assessment of whether individuals need leadership. As you will recall, John believes leadership is primarily a technical responsibility and that intelligent people do not need close personal contact to do their jobs. These assumptions will influence what happens next at Invest.

In a recent extensive study of some ninety outstanding leaders, Bennis and Nanus identified four major strategies or competencies that all ninety leaders seemed to exhibit (1) management of attention through vision, (2) meaning through communication, (3) trust through positioning, and (4) deployment of self through positive self-regard and the Wallenda factor.

The outstanding leaders of the Bennis and Nanus study commanded the attention of their followers and organizations by establishing and communicating a *vision* about where the organization should go, what it should be, and what was needed to achieve it. As Bennis and Nanus suggest, "All ninety people interviewed has an agenda, an unparalleled concern with outcome. Leaders are the most results-oriented individuals in the world, and results get attention.... The visions these various leaders connived seemed to bring about a confidence on the part of the employees, a confidence that instilled in them a belief that they were capable of performing the necessary acts." Bennis and Nanus further suggested that successful leaders not only caught the attention of others but also paid attention to others, underscoring the essential interactional relationship between leaders and followers.

The second strategy, the management of meaning through *communication,* relates to the conscious effort the leaders made to communicate so their meanings would become the meanings of every organizational level. These excellent leaders were concerned not only with what should be done but also with how to develop messages that conveyed that vision. Bennis and Nanus state, "Getting the message across unequivocally at every level is an absolute key. Basically it is what the creative process is all about and what, once again, separates the managers from the leaders." Management of meaning rests on well-developed communication competencies and an understanding of the process of organizational communication. Without competencies and process of understanding, effective leadership is problematic.

Trust as a strategy is hard to define. Bennis and Nanus describe trust as the "glue that maintains organizational integrity" The leaders in the Bennis and Nanus study were trusted because they were constant, predictable, and reliable. They position themselves as worthy of trust by exhibiting personal stability even while encouraging change and innovation. They helped their organizations develop a sense of identify and integrity. This sense of direction is considered by Bennis and Nanus to be fundamental to their effectiveness.

Finally, the effective leaders in the study liked themselves and other people. They did not focus on failure but viewed mistakes as learning opportunities and challenges. they were like farmed tightrope walker Karl Wallenda, who until shortly on walking, never falling. Bennis and Nanus contend that the "Wallenda factor" in leadership is the ability to focus on success, not failure, and to frame our behaviour in terms of the goal, not every detail of the process.

The strategy of positive self-regard and regard for others is closely related to our description of developing communication competencies for organizational excellence. The relationship between regard and developing communication competencies is made clear when Bennis and Nanus sum up positive self-regard as three major factors: "knowledge of one's strengths, the capacity to nurture and develop those strengths, and the ability to discern the fit between one's strengths and weaknesses and the organization's needs." They continue, "In the case of our ninety leaders, they used five key skills: (1) The ability to accept people as they are, not as you would like them to be... (2) The capacity to approach relationships and problems in terms of the present rather than the past... (3) The ability to treat those who are close to you with the same courteous attention that you extend to strangers and causal acquaintances.. (4) The ability to trust others, even if the risk seems great... (5) The ability to do without constant approval and recognition from others."

Recent research by Eric Eisenberg lends support to the Bennis and Nanus contention that generating vision is an important leadership responsibility. Eisenberg propose *strategic ambiguity* as an organizational communication strategy that promotes unity while maintaining sufficient individual freedom to ensure flexibility, creativity, and change. Eisenberg argues that divergent organizational goals cannot always be resolved through the development of specific consensus from all organizational members. He proposes that

> Ambiguity is used strategically to foster agreement on abstractions without limiting specific interpretations....Focusing on organizational symbolism casts leadership in a new light as well. While a primary responsibility of leaders is to make meanings for followers and to infuse employees with values and purpose the process of doing so is less one of consensus-making and more one of using language strategically to express values at a level of abstraction at which agreement can occur...Effective leaders ambiguity strategically to encourage creativity and guard against the acceptance of one standard way of viewing organization reality.

Organizational goal and mission statements, communication rules, and organizational stories and myths are all examples of strategies ambiguity influences by leaders. An excellent example of strategic ambiguity comes from the recurring theme to "do what's right, not what's written of a certain large computer manufacturer.

What's "right" subject to varying interpretations across the organization. The leadership imperative, however, is to take action and personal responsibility, a value with high consensus even though specific interpretations often vary dramatically. In fact, conflict frequently occurs in this genrally healthy organization over "what is right" and "who should decide."

We have discussed autocratic, participative, and laissez-faire or avoidance strategies for leadership. We have also described strategies for the communication of vision, management of meaning through communication, management of trust, and management of positive self-regard and regard for others. We will now describe specific communication tactics used for each of these strategic orientations.

Communication tactics for leadership

Leadership tactics can be described ad the communication behaviors used to support authoritarian participative, and avoidance preferences as well as to establish vision, mange meaning, generate trust, and communicate regard and success orientation. Specific tactics are influenced by individual preferences and strategies, by communication competencies of leaders and followers, and by overall organizational values and expectations about how leadership[works. Military organizations, for example, encourage authoritarian leadership, whereas organizations, involved in research and development of new products usually stress more participative styles. Still others reflect a mix of leadership approaches representing the diversity of people and personalities wlfo work together. It is important to understand that as with conflict tactic, the choice of specific leadership tactics illustrates the interactive nature of relationships. Both leaders and followers are involved in complex tactical interactions influenced by individual preferences and strategic objectives as well as the needs of a particular situation.

It is not possible to list or useful for out personal sensitivity and out skill development, however, to identify several frequently used communication tactics. Figure presents excerpts from group problem-solving situations in which the identified group leader illustrates a particular leadership tactic. Each example is accompanied by a description of

The tactic it represents, and tactics are grouped into authoritarian, participative, avoidance, vision-setting, meaning-management, trust-generating, and positive regard and success categories.

Power bases for leaders

Preferences for leadership, strategic objectives, and communication tactics all contribute to how leaders influence followers. Yet behaviours alone do not adequately explain how one individual is recognized as leader whereas another is not. We have all seen individuals who are recognized as leaders exhibit almost identical behaviours as those who never achieve leadership recognition.

Frequently the difference in who is a leader and who is not is a subtle matter of credibility-a credibility that enables one person to be more influential than another. This credibility is commonly referred to as *power* or the power bases of the leader.

The concept of power can best be understood as an interactive process. In other words, power does not exist in a vacuum, but rather as people interact with one another. Form this perspective power can be understood interact with one another. From this perspective power can be understood as the influence an individual has over another as a result of dependency on the powerful person. To understand this interaction it is helpful to think about some of the power bases available to leaders. John french and Bertram Raven have given us a useful description of five power types; legitimate, reward, coercive, referent and expert. We will also discuss connection power.

Legitimate power comes from the positions, titles, or roles people occupy. Supervisors have legitimate power over subordinates. As such, certain rights and responsibilities are "legitimately" defined and generally understood by group members. Disagreement can surround the ability of the "legitimate " leader, yet most agree that certain leadership responsibilities accompany the position. For example, virtually every president of the United States has supporters and critics, yet despite these diverse opinions few would disagree that the individual is legitimately the president.

Reward power is based on the leaders control and distribution of tangible and intangible reward resources. A leader can influence with the promise of rewards only as long as those rewards are within the leader's control and perceived by followers as rewarding. Many people attempt to influence with rewards that other do not find important or influential. Many supervisors believe, for example, that money is the primary reward for good performance, although considerable research suggests that communication contact with supervisors is one o the most sought-after of all subordinate rewards. Interestingly enough, communication interaction is more often controlled by supervisors that money or other tangible benefits.

Coercive power can be understood as the sanctions or punishments within the control of the leader. Coercive power is the ability to punish for not complying with influence attempts. To be effective, coercive power must not be threatened beyond what the leader is willing to administer. All of us have seen people lose credibility by threatening sanctions or punishment that were not within the control of the one making the threats. Although reward power can be exercised by virtually anyone, coercive power is related to the role or legitimate position an individual occupies.

For example, a peer can threaten to get another peer fired, but although unpleasant, the threat is generally not considered coercive power. When a supervisor makes the same threat, the influence attempt takes on an entirely different meaning.

Referent power is a result of others identifying with the leader. It is a power base that is only indirectly related to the leader's overt influence attempts. Referent power comes from the desire of others to use the leader as a "reference' of from others seeking to imitate the leader's behaviors from actions of the leader's desire for them to do so. Referent power results from actions of the leader. yet the leader cannot directly exercise referent power-it is assigned by others.

Expert or information power rest on what the leader knows as a result of organization interaction pr areas of technical specialty. As such, expert power does not require legitimate power for the expert to be influential. Expert power can be used without coercive power and often contributes to the development of referent power. Expert power is considered to be important for organizational excellence and is ideally the basis of effective influence attempts.

Connection power is the influence leaders have as a result of who they know sand the support they have from others in the organization. Generally conceived of as support from others in power, connection power also comes from followers. Supervisors and mangers, for example are generally in better influence positions when follower "connections" are supportive. In turn, group members ae more influential when their leaders are "connected: to others in the organization. connection power is understood by observing communication networks and how individuals are linked throughout the organization.

Situational analysis for leadership

Understanding the situations or circumstances requiring leadership is fundamental for effectiveness. The ability to assess thoughtfully the requirements of the problem and the group attempting its solutions contributes to the selection of effective strategies and tactics for leadership.

The ability to communicate vision is related to the ability to generate vision based on sound problem analysis. Communicating outcomes is related to knowing where an organization should go and having a concept of how it can get there. In other words, good problem-solving and analysis skills are fundamental for effective leadership. Analysis skill help defence problems, generate solutions and contribute to the selection of influence strategies appropriate for leadership. Analysis skills cannot be separated from influence strategies for effectiveness. The individual who thoroughly understands a problem may not be able to influence others if communication strategies and tactics are carelessly chosen. On the other hand, we have concern for individuals who are so adapt at persuasive communication that they convince groups to follow courses of action that are ill conceived or ill advised.

John Mitchell's experience at Invest is a good example. Chances are john has the technical expertise to lead the laboratory to significant technical accomplishments. No one doubts his ability to analyze technical problems. Yet John is close to failure as the managers or the laboratory. His situational analysis is only partially complete He understands the technical direction he wants but has not communicated his vision to others and does not see any need for that type of "sales' pitch. John's communication behaviors do not reflect his technical excellence. his dilemma illustrates what can happen when problem analysis is not coupled with appropriate communication behaviors.

Increasing leadership effectiveness

We can describe the communication competencies needed to increase leadership capabilities as an expansion of those competencies necessary for interpersonal and conflict management effectiveness. The knowledge, sensitivity, skills, and values identified and developed in previous chapters are all important for effective leadership, especially if we take the position that organizations need leadership from all positions levels.

As we have previously suggested, effective leaders understand the problems facing their group and have skill in helping diverse individuals approach common problems. Effective leaders participate in group efforts and encourage others to participate by being open-minded and exhibiting supportive behaviors. Effective leaders, however, will help groups make decisions when consensus is unlikely. finally, effective leaders empower others by sharing success and credit.

Self-awareness is a key to leadership effectiveness. Understanding personal preferences, behaviors, and problem situations if fundamental to discovering why some leadership efforts succeed while others fail. Return for a moment to your personal theory of leadership. What does it tell you about your personal leadership strengths and weakness" What competencies need further development? When have you been most successful?

In an effort to help you increase your leadership effectiveness, we will describe an important concept of principle leadership; identify task, procedural, and interpersonal leadership responsibilities; and discuss leadership in group setting by identifying barriers to effective group decision making and by proposing how to plan for leadership in a group setting. Finally, knowledge, sensitivity, skill, and value competencies will be applied in the workshop section of the chapter.

Principled leadership

In their extensive study of successful teams, Carl Karson and Frank LaFasto identified principled leadership as one of the core characteristics of why successful teams develop. According to Larson and LaFasto, principled leadership provides a consisted message, has a perspective for unleashing talent, practice ago suppression and creates leaders.

Larson and LaFasto found that "effective team leaders begin by establishing a vision of the future. In the most common language, this need was articulated a s the clear. Elevating goals. Such a goal, or vision, is hallmark of effective leaders. They articulate what an organization can and should become, or what a team can or should accomplish. Furthermore, they articulate the team's goal in such a way as to inspire a desire for and eventual commitment to the accomplishment of the goal. The goal, or vision, is seen as worthwhile, making team members eager to be a part of its achievement." In other words, principled leadership establishes and communicates a vision that create change by unleashing the talent of team members.

In thinking about increasing our own leadership effectiveness, we question what qualities and behaviors are most likely to generate this commitment to vision and overall leadership success. The work of Larson and LaFasto provides insight:

> A content analysis of our research data yield a consistent message that focused on how team leaders generated enthusiasm, a bias for action,and a commitment to the team's objective among team members. The single most distinguishing feature of the effective leaders in our data base was their ability to establish, and lead by, guiding principles. these principles represented day-to-day performance

> standards. They represented what all team members, including the team leader, should expect from one another on a day-to-day basis. The principles identified by our sample created three natural categories of expectations: (1) what the team should expect of the team leader; (2) what the team leader should except from each team member, and each team member should expect from one another; and (3) leadership principles that established a supportive decision-making climate in which team members could take risks.

Not only did the successful leaders of the Larson and LaFasto work unleash talent through the use of guiding principles but they also suppressed individual ego displays for themselves and the team. Team members were active participants in shaping he destiny of the team, and this active participation contributed to leadership not only for the team but also within the team. In sum we can sat that effective leadership promotes the development of leadership in others. Think for a moment about your own leadership attempts. Which of the Larson and LaFasto principles did you use? Which were missing? Would you add others to the list? Next we will consider how effective leaders use principled leadership for task, procedural, and interpersonal responsibilities.

Identifying constructive communication behaviors for leadership

Task responsibilities

Whether leading a major corporation or leading a

group in a class project, leaders have task, procedural, and interpersonal responsibilities. in the task area, leaders are responsible for facilitating problem analysis, idea generation, idea evaluation, solution generation , and decision implemntion. Leaders need to stimulate creativity and urge people to push the boundaries of their thinking. Effective leaders encourage team members to listen actively to others and expand good ideas. Leaders are responsible for promoting focused and in-depth investigation of ideas and critically evaluating all aspects of a problem. Leaders help the group address the accuracy of their information, evaluate information sources, apply information carefully to defined problems, and develop solution criteria. Which of the principles would you apply to task responsibilities? What types of communication skills are required? Can you understand the importance of communication competency for effective leadership?

Procedural responsibilities

Leaders also are responsible for procedures such as goal setting, agenda making, discussion clarification, and both consensus and disagreement identification. Leaders must be able to introduce ideas, give direction, and call for action. They ask for ideas and the participation of team member. Leaders remind groups of agendas and goals and generally organize group activities. Leaders actively listen as well as offer explanations for their own and others' verbalizations and behaviors. Recall the description in Chapter 6 of communication skills important for group participation. All of these skills and more apply to leadership responsibilities. In effect, we can say that leaders and team members alike must develop key interaction process skills for effective group efforts. Again review the guiding principles in figure. Which of the principles apply to procedural responsibilities? What might you add?

Interpersonal responsibilities

Finally, leaders make significant contributions to the interpersonal dynamics of groups. Leaders contribute to participation, group climate, and conflict management, As Larson and LaFasto have suggested, effective leaders generate and environment in which team members can achieve excellence because they have the confidence to take risks. Confidence to take risk comes from the supportive climate of effective interpersonal relationships. Leaders are responsible for reflecting feelings and supporting others, empathizing, and stopping personal attacks or other counterproductive individual or group behaviors. What guiding principles should a leader adopt for interpersonal responsibilities? What skill are most important?

In summary we say that leaders affect how the task is accomplished, how people are supported within the group, and what processes and procedures the group uses to achieve its objectives. Group members also share these responsibilities, but the leader remains influential in guiding task, procedural, and interpersonal contributions.

Leading the group meeting

A frequent test of leadership capability comes in leading meetings. Research tells us that many organizational members spend from 40 to 95 percent of their time in meetings. The results of these meetings are crucial to overall organizational excellence. It is fair to say that meetings are one of the most important communication activities in most organizations. It is also likely that for most people, meetings offer a promising yet underused opportunity to exhibit leadership ability.

But how effective are most meetings? Think about your own experiences. Are the meetings you attend well run and productive? How could they be improved? A recent survey of *Fortune* 500 executives listed meetings as necessary but among their top time-wasters in organizational life. A visit to almost any large organization finds individual schedules packed with meetings and complaints that little gets done because people are always in meetings.

With meetings a ripe opportunity for exhibiting leadership, the question is what we can do to contribute to effective meetings. First, it is important to understand what typically goes wrong in meetings and what role leadership can play in preventing and correcting problems. Second, leaders need to understand the basics of preparing for an running effective meetings.

Barriers to effective meetings

Leland Brandford has suggested several barriers to successful meetings. Specifically, he contends that meetings fail to reach their potential because of lack of communication skills, apathy; conflict within the group; and reactions against the task that include avoidance, fear of making decisions, and fear of taking responsibility. Members get impatient, attack the ideas of others, and generally contribute to polarized positions. Although we can argue that these barriers are everyone's responsibility, most would agree that effective leadership is crucial to their elimination.

Preparation for the group meeting

Three general stages of the process must be understood fro a leader to contribute to productive group outcomes. These stages are meeting preparation, the meeting itself, and meeting evaluation Each stage requires personnel communication competency and the ability to assess the communication competency of group participants.

Preparation for any meeting should first include identifying the purpose of the meeting and the composition of members needed to fulfill that purpose. Many organizational meetings are worthless because the purpose is ill defined and the appropriate organizational members are not present. Questions to ask while establishing the purpose include these" Is a meeting the best way to discuss this problem or disseminate this information? Who should be included for maximum effectiveness? How much can we hope to accomplish at one time? Meeting preparation also includes finding a time and place appropriate for a well-defined propose, Factors to be considered included convenience, privacy, and appropriate accommodations.

Meeting preparation also includes developing some type of agenda, informing potential members of the reasons for meeting, and preparing such items as handouts and audiovisual materials. But meeting preparation should include communication preparation as well. Thoughtful leaders think about communication approaches, potential problems, and how best to encourage equality participation. Communication preparation may include thinking about successes and failures in past meetings and asking others to critique the effectiveness of past leadership attempts. It aslo should include any introductory remarks or information for which the leader is responsible.

Conducting the group meeting

As stated in the previous section, leadership responsibilities include task, procedural, and interpersonal dimensions. When conducting a meeting, the effective leader is continually assessing tactic appropriate to balance all three. Nowhere in organizational life is there more need for well-developed communication competencies. Leaders are responsible for beginning meetings and establishing focus. Leaders influence the procedures by which the meeting is run, whether those procedures are informal or formal. Although all group members can and usually should be encouraged to take responsibility for the group's climate and interpersonal relationships, leaders influence interpersonal relationships by the type of participation they encourage, by the support they give to differences of opinion by the manner in which they deal with conflict, and by the control they establish over a variety of disruptive influences. Finally, leaders are primarily responsible for guiding the group to goal achievement or determining why goals cannot be accomplished within the meeting setting.

Leaders are not, however, totally responsible or the success or failure of the group. Successes depends on the abilities and wiliness of all involved to participate. Leadership can enhance the success of a group but cannot alone generate good problem solving without motivation participation and competent group members.

Meeting evaluation

Leaders are in a good position to evaluate thoughtfully the results of group meetings. In fact, effective leaders frequently assess themselves, the quality of the group's effort, and the process by which these efforts were achieved. Only through this continuing assessment can leadership excellence be maintained. Effective leaders test the productivity of meetings not simply by whether decisions were reached but also by whether members actually followed through on their commitments. In addition, effective leaders evaluate the quality of group decisions once implemented and tested by time. Chances are all of us have been in groups that reach decisions on problems, only to have no one really take initiative for implementation. These groups appear a harmonious but in reality are not effective. Leaders of such groups appear harmonious but in reality are not effective. Leaders of such groups can easily mislead themselves into thinking they are productive even through the evidence suggests little ever gets done. Effective leaders know the importance of evaluation not only the meeting itself but also the outcomes and results of decisions or commitments.

11 Groups in Organisational Conflict

Most of us have been in groups in which tensions and conflict made us uncomfortable or blocked problem solving. It is hoped that most of us also belonged to groups in which conflict contributed to new and better ways of doing things, actually strengthening the groups ability to work together. Think for a moment about these experience. What made the difference? How did you feel and behave in these differing circumstances?

Individuals in group conflicts

Earlier we described a variety of orientations, predispositions, and styles; strategic objectives, and communication tactics. As you would expect, these orientations, objectives, and behaviors can contribute to conflict when diverse individuals participate in groups. Group members also play task, maintenance, and self-centered roles. It is easy to understand why self-centered roles and inappropriate balances of task and maintenance roles are a possible source of group conflict. Additionally, although most organizations talk about the importance of teamwork, rewards usually recognize individual versus group efforts.

Members of a work team, for example, will be asked to collaborate, yet each knows that merit salary increases will reflect how they compare to each other, not how they produce as a group. This seeming contradiction is another source of work group conflict.

Procedural conflict

Most types of organizational groups conflict over procedures or ways of doing things. How the group organized the process of decision making who accepts responsibility, or what happens when responsibilities are not carried out can all contribute to tension and conflict within groups. Most of you have experienced this procedural conflict when preparing a project for a class. Some group members preferred majority rule, others worked for genuine consensus, and still others attempted to force their positions or opinions on the entire group.

Interpersonal issues

One of the most common types of group conflict emerges when all members do not fairly or equally perform their responsibilities or make contributions to the group. The necessity to "carry" a member of the team raises tension and disrupts group cohesiveness. Groups also have interpersonal power dashes clashes between and among members who seek influence and control. Powerful members produce conflict when attempting to force group members to take sides in essentially interpersonal disputes. We have all observed two individuals disagreeing or disparaging one another in front of the group. We often suspect that their disagreements have little or nothing to do with the issues at hand but reflect ongoing difficulties in the relationship. Unfortunately, they introduce tension and counterproductive behaviors into what might otherwise be an effective setting.

Substantive issues

The very reason for forming groups in organizations can contribute to group conflict. we have said that organizations should utilize the energy of diverse individuals to establish effective ways of doing things or to challenge existing processes in favor of new and better efforts. In effect, we are saying that organizations should encourage conflicts of ideas that contribute to excellence. Individuals normally and productively can differ about positions, interests, approaches, or problems. Groups, therefore, can be expected to have conflicts over issues, ideas, or tasks.

Groupthink

As is true in interpersonal conflict, group conflict can range from highly productive to counterproductive. Most of us have been present at a meeting where displays of anger blocked effective problem solving effectiveness.

Surface harmony, or the absence of productive conflict, can block group effectiveness when critical thinking is absent, resulting in ill-conceived courses of action. Irving janis has called the surface harmony frequently associated with highly cohesive groups groupthink, or the tendency of groups to suspend critical thinking and to adopt proposed solutions too quickly. Groups in danger of groupthink overestimate their own capabilities, seek information that supports their point of view and avoid or discount contradictory ideas. Have you ever participated in groupthink? what happened? How can group members decide if they genuinely agree or are exhibiting groupthink tendencies? Our discussion of a format for productive conflict will provide some possible answers..

Group conflict management processes

Group conflict is so important in organizations that a variety of processes for management have become commonplace. These processes are typically described as negotiation, bargaining, mediation, forcing and arbitration. Although this chapter will not describe each of these processes in detail, your awareness that they are frequently used becomes part of your knowledge competency for group participation.

Negotiation is a common process in groups. Generally speaking, negotiation can be understood as a broad process involving discussions between and among individuals who are interdependent and need to come together for a decision or course of action. Groups negotiate procedures and issues with expected give and take among members. The negotiation process is frequently associated with the need to compromise effectively. The next section of his chapter describes a concept of principled negotiation that supports productive conflict.

Bargaining is a more structured form of negotiations. Bargaining usually involves the presentation of of fairly specific proposals for the purpose of achieving a working agreement on particular issues. You are probably familiar with collective bargaining as it applies to labor and management group interactions. Yet burning has numerous other organizational applications. At budget time groups may be asked to present very specific proposals for money. Representatives from each group may be asked to negotiate or bargain for fixed resources. In some cases the rules for these exchanges will be well defined, whereas in other the process is more open-ended. Regardless of the formality, bargaining is an established conflict resolution procedure in many organizations.

Mediation is another possible group conflict management process. In mediation a designated individual guides the negotiations or bargaining efforts of the groups in conflict. Mediation us utilized when negotiations are deadlocked or tensions so high that a designated leader us desirable. When mediation fails the designated leader frequently has to rely on forcing or making a decision that the group must accept. Obviously, for mediation or forcing to be effective, the designated leader must have credibility with the opposing factions and responsibility and authority appropriate to the task. Generally speaking, mediators are members of the group or organization involved in the process.

Finally, when negotiation, bargaining or mediation fails, organizations can manage group conflict with third-party arbitration. Arbitration usually involves an outside negotiator who resolves differences with formally established procedures. labor-management disputes have been subjects of arbitration as have a variety of legally related cases. Arbitration frequently results in ill will because of the forced nature of resolving the conflict.

Fortunately most of us will work in groups that manage conflict through collaboration and negotiation. We know from experience that effectiveness is more likely to occur when group members voluntarily solve their own disputes than whcn leaders or an outside individual must take charge. The need, therefore, is to devolop an understanding of how to engage in conflict productively. The next section of this chapter contributes to our competencies by describing supportive climates, ethical behaviors, and principled negotiation for conflict. The section concludes with a recommended format for productive conflict.

Productively engaging in conflict

Specifically, we have attempted to develop knowledge, sensitivity, and skills important for communication competence during conflict. The underlying assumption for this development has been that conflict can be productive and can make a valuable contribution to individuals and organizations. In other words, not only is conflict inevitable, but also, when productively managed, it is often desirable.

Before we think specifically about possible positive outcomes of conflict, review again the conflicts you identified earlier in this chapter and the Middlesex insurance case. Were there positive outcomes from your personal conflicts? What do John and the entire department have to gain from productive resolution of their problem? How was conflict valuable in either your personal experience or the Middlesex case?

In general we can say that a major value of conflict is its stimulus for creativity. Conflict with others forces us to evaluate and assess issues and problems. When productively managed, this evaluation can stimulate new and creative solutions that may not have emerged without competing perspectives. For examples, most of us have habitual or routine ways of doing things. Frequently we do not even think about new approaches until someone challenges our effectiveness. Productive conflict can help keep us from getting in a rut. Conflict can restructure our relationships-a fact many of us fear and resist. Yet conflict can bring relationships up to date and strengthen them by addressing underlying problems and working for solutions. Both individually and organizationally, productive conflict can help us analyze goals and find effective means of achieving them.

When we adopt the perspective that conflict can be valuable, we then begin to focus our knowledge, sensitivity, and skills toward conflict as a productive process. We think about what atmosphere is best for conflict, what contributes to ethical behaviors during conflict, and finally what types of problem-solving processes support productive conflict outcomes.

Supportive climates, ethical behaviors, and principled negotiation

Creating an environment in which individuals feel secure and encouraged to seek good solutions is a difficult yet important task. The quality of the problem-solving environment is closely linked to considerations of what constitutes ethical communication behaviors during conflict. This subtle but critical relationship between supportive climates and the quality of human interaction is well described by Paul Keller and Charles Brown in their interpersonal ethic for communication. Keller and Brown suggest that people will be able to reach their potential only when they are psychologically free-not fearful of disagreement-and when their beliefs, opinions, and values are acceptable in their interactions with others.

Organizations annually spend millions of dollars training personnel in problem solving and conflict management with the hope that this training will contribute to productive organizational outcomes. And yet the out-comes from conflict often are influenced not only by the skills and abilities of the individual conflict participants but also by the overall organizational climate, which contributes to either supportiveness or detensiveness.

Organizational climates that produce defensiveness are characterized by inaccurate perceptions of motives, values, and emotions of those in conflict. Lack Gibb, in a classic study of behaviors individuals perceive as threatening, discovered that "increases in defensive behavior were correlated positively with losses in efficiency in communicate9on. Specifically, distortions became greater when defensive states existed in the groups. Gibb concluded that there are characteristic behaviors of defensive groups that are distinctly different from the characteristic behaviors in supportive groups.

Evaluation versus problem description

Defensive climates are described by Gibb as being evaluative, whereas supportive environments are characterized by problem description. The supervisor who identifies the "bad attitude" or "low commitment" of a subordinate may not fully understand how this evaluative approach contributes to a predictably defensive subordinate reaction. On the other hand, the supervisor who describes concern for a subordinates absenteeism is describing a problem both the supervisor and subordinate can readily observe and approach-very different from the subjective assessment of attitudes. In summary the descriptive approach attempts to fit our words as nearly as possible to our experience of reality through descriptive, non-judgmental terms and by avoiding strong, emotion-laden words.

Control versus problem orientation

Defensiveness also is produced through attempts to control the behavior and responses of others. Although enforcing compliance may get short-term results, it rarely builds long-term commitment. Problem orientation is the supportive climate opposite to control. Specifically, problem orientation assumes a collaborative approach to solutions with particular emphasis on the participation of those being asked to make behavior changes. One of the more difficult tasks for many new managers is to encourage participation from those who either need to make behavior changes or are most affected by them. Inexperienced managers frequently learn that attempts to control subordinate behaviors result in the need for time-consuming behavior monitoring. Their more experienced counterparts have learned that subordinates are more likely to keep commitments in which they participate.

Most of us can understand the problem orientation approach in our own behavior. Try to determine when your commitments is greater-when you participate in a decision or when that decision is made for you. For most of us the answer is relatively simple; We put more time and energy into our own commitments.

Strategy versus spontaneity

Although we all operate from strategic objectives in conflict, defensiveness is produced when we are perceived by others to be engaging in manipulative behaviors. Organizational strategies for "selling" unpopular decisions often produce a defensiveness based on the belief that manipulation is a fundamental form of disrespect-Spontaneity, the opposite of strategy, is reflected in behaviors that make real motives plain and generate a trust that straightforward and honest interactions are taking place. This trust level is fundamental for long-term effectiveness. In fact, Warren Bennis and Burt Nanus, in their research on leaders, suggest that trust in their constancy is one of the fundamental distinguishing characteristics of highly successful leaders. Furthermore, as Joseph DeVito suggests, straightforward and honest interactions facilitate the individual's freedom of choice through accurate information-a requirement in his view for ethical interpersonal communication.

Neutrality versus empathy

Gibb found that productive groups empathically supported their members rather than assuming a rational neutrality based on "pure" objectivity. Productive groups also were characterized by the acceptance of others with different values and beliefs. This empathic support is closely related to the Keller and Brown notion of an interpersonal ethic for communication based on psychological freedom to express opinions and beliefs. Thinking again about our personal behavior, most of us would agree that it is more comfortable to express disagreement when we know we will be throughtfully heard than when we expect personal attack or discounting. Also. for most of us, constructively expressing disagreement is more likely to occur when we feel supported in our right to do so.

Superiority versus equality

In general, defensive groups are more likely than supportive groups to have members intent on asserting superiority and exhibiting an unwillingness to participate equally in problem solving. In fact, defensive climates are often characterized by individuals believing they really do not have enough in common with others to make communication possible. Although differences in individuals exist, supportive individuals and groups stress commonalities while respecting numerous and diverse contributions to solutions.

Certainty versus provisionalism

Defensive groups, more than their supportive counterparts, are likely to have members who are certain and dogmatic about their positions. Supportive individuals are more provisional or open to experimentation in behavior, attitudes, and ideas. The provisional individual is investigative and problem oriented rather than polarized into either-or positions. The provisional approach seeks numerous alternatives in order to find the most appropriate solution to a given problem. Again, this support for the generation of alternatives is fundamental to individual choice and ethical communication.

Ethical communication behaviours

The supportive conditions as described by Gibb are closely aligned to notions of ethical conflict behaviors as described by Gary Kreps and Barbara Thornton. Specifically, Kreps and

Thornton believe ethical conflict behaviors are exhibited when the individual stays with the issue at hand without hidden agendas; contrasts reasonable, logical arguments rather than arguments designed to discount and devalue others, and keeps an open mind to new ideas while avoiding a win-at-all-costs, attitude. In other words, ethical communication behaviors generate an environment in which individuals have freedom of expression and also have adequate information to make free, informed choices. Put another way, the value of productive conflict is to stimulate creativity in individuals, groups, and organizations. That creativity is most likely to emerge of we are personally safe, if we are open to many suggestions and viewpoints, and if we honestly seek the best solution from among numerous alternatives.

Principled negotiation

Principled negotiation is based on ethical communication behaviors and supportive climates. First introduced by Roger Fisher and William Ury, principled negotiation is a strategy for groups of individuals in conflict both to express their needs and to search for alternatives that meet diverse needs. The strategy supports ethical behavior by separating people from the problem and focusing on interests, not positions. Group members are asked to develop options for mutual gain based on mutual interests. Additionally objective criteria are used to evaluate options so all parties to the conflict can determine the fairness of decisions.

Principled negotiation is based on the assumption that we should express disagreements and react to them with a spirit of inquiry and supportiveness rather than defensiveness. During principled negotiations group members express concern for one another even when issue and position disagreements are obvious. Groups engaging in principled negotiation describe needs and interests in common and avoid rigid, polarized positions. Utilizing common needs and interests as a basis, groups develop options that can be evaluated with agreed-upon objective criteria. Once evaluation has been completed, groups engaging in principled negotiation can arrive at decisions with a high likelihood of broad support.

A format for productive conflict

Individuals who observe or participate in productive conflicts frequently characterize them as good problem-solving processes. And indeed, that is exactly what productive conflict is. Earlier in the chapter conflict was defined as frustration stimulated by competing responses or alternatives to a particular situation. When that frustration is resolved to the mutual satisfaction of involved parties and to the needs of the issues, good problem solving has occurred. The following format for productive conflicts is a basic problem-solving format. Based on the concepts of supportive climates, ethical behaviors, and principled negotiation, it is designed to integrate all of our competencies-knowledge, sensitivity, skills, and values-into a productive conflict management process.

The format

Self-analysis of the issues. When we are experiencing perceived and felt conflict, the time is right to do an in-depth self-analysis about the problem. Can we describe the conflicts in terms that represent observable behaviors or events to all parties? What are the limits of our understanding of the problem? What types of solutions can we purpose? Who needs to change or make a decision? What can we support in resolution strategies and what types of results are clearly not acceptable? Also, what are the power issues, roles, and relationships of the parties involved? Finally, what are our presonal responsibilities for this conflict?

Setting a meeting to work on the problem. Productive conflict occurs in a climate in which all participants feel supported. The setting of the meeting beforehand and the environment of the meeting itself are critical to this supportive climate. Generally, speaking, all parties involved in conflict should be notified in advance about the issue for discussion. Although this will sometimes produce anticipation stress, mental preparation can occur only when everyone knows the agenda. Also, the emotional impact of conflict can be lessened and trust levels increased when people dont feel surprised by a conflict. Commitment to agreements is greater if parties have time to think about the problem and their input and limits. In addition, the meeting environment should be conducive to the free exchange of ideas-usually private and on relatively neutral ground.

Individuals using the power position of their private office may actually inhibit real problem solving. Finally, adequate time for full discussion should be allotted, with the timing of the meeting as convenient as possible for all participants.

Defining the problem. Effective conflict outcomes occur in solving the basic problem rather than finding solutions. to surface issues or discovering vastly differing descriptions of the problem. Conflict participants should be encouraged to define the problem fully before any discussion of solution strategies. Problems often are poorly described because of underlying tension in the setting and a desire to get the confrontation over with as soon as possible. Clarification of the problem-through self-disclosure and active questioning-is essential to productive problem solving.

Developing solutions. We are often relived to be "getting through this problem" and neglect to look comprehensively art approaches and solutions. In the development of solutions it is important to think broadly about all alternatives, even those that seem to have little immediate merit. Better and longer-lasting solutions will emerge from broad rather than narrow perspectives of alternatives. All conflict participants should be encouraged to participate in solution generation. In fact, if a critically involved party to a dispute cannot offer a single solution, it may be better to adjourn the meeting temporarily and let that person consider what he or she might suggest. Forcing a decision on a nonparticipative individual may result in little commitment or sometimes actual sabotage of the solution. Ultimately, of course, action must be taken. However, all parties must recognize the potential impact of a decision with varying ranges of agreement and commitment.

Narrowing the choices for action. Decisions should be discussed in light of the defined problem issues. Often decisions made with broad agreement fail because the participants have not linked their intended actions to the actual problem. It behavior changes is required on the part of some but not all participants, particular care should be taken that the affected individuals participate in narrowing the choices for action. They should be encouraged to select options to which they can commit, although these options can be rejected by others if they do not meet acceptable standards. When individuals who need to change their behavior make commitments to change that they have helped generate, the long-term possibilities for successful conflict resolution have been enhanced.

Commitment to solutions. Agreement on a solution or approach to the problem should occur only after the parties assess how that solution addresses the identified problem, whether individuals can support the decision, if those most affected have participated in the decision, and whether the solution is workable and can be implemented. Commitment to the solution comes through developing an implementation plan. Who is going to do what and in what time frame? How is the solution going to be evaluated? Is everyone clear about what we think this solution will accomplish and also what it cannot do? Finally, can we predict from this experience whether we have a solution that will work? If so, what were the keys to this outcomes? If not, what were the barriers we could not surmount?

Monitoring the process. A real key to long-term conflict management is effective implementation of agreed-upon solutions. Effective conflict out-comes are encouraged when participants establish how they will monitor the implementation plan and when they will meet again to assess how it is working. This follow-up builds accountability into the process and also allows for celebration when solutions are working and meeting problem needs.

Although no process, set of skills, or body of knowledge will free individuals, groups, or entire organizations from the reality of conflict, the knowledge, sensitiveness skills, and values of conflict participants directly influence the productivity of conflict outcomes. Effective organizational communicators know they bear responsibilities to monitor continually their own ability and support that process for others. In particular, effective conflict outcomes help individuals improve their oraganizational relationships and are an important organizational mechanism for good decision making and adaptation to change.

12 The Individual in Organisational Conflict

Organizations bring together diverse individuals, some of whom approach conflict as you would and others with very different preferences. The various predispositions, skills, and abilities of individuals in organizations influence how organizational conflict occurs. Sensitivity to these differences in central to becoming a competent communicator within a complex environment.

Sensitivity to our own preferences and behaviors helps us develop sensitivity to differences among people. One of the best ways to develop that sensitivity is to examine our own preferences in conflicts that have been important to us. The questionnaire is designed to increase your awareness of your individual preferences and predispositions for conflict.

Upon completion of the questionnaire in you will have short profiles of three conducts you saw as important to you. These profiles are organized around conflict scholar Kenneth Thomas's basic components of individual conflict behavior: orientation/style, strategic objectives, and tactics. You will want to refer to your profiles as we discuss each of the behavior components.

Orientations, or predispositions, for conflict are the balances individuals try to make between satisfying their personal needs and goals and satisfying the needs and goals of others in the conflict. These orientations or predispositions are commonly referred to as conflict styles. Strategic objectives are a combination of balancing the individual preferences for conflict styles with

what the individual sees as feasible outcomes in a particular situation. Behavior choices, known as tactics, are specific communication choices that-are influenced by both orientation and style and strategic objectives.

Orientations/Predispositions/Styles

Prominent conflict researchers such as Leonard Berkowitz, Robert Blake and Jane Mouton, Jay Hall, and Kenneth Thomas all support the notion that individuals have behavioral orientations predispositions or styles for handling conflict. Researchers further conclude that individuals have an order of preference among the styles that ultimately influences communication choices. In other words, an individual has a dominant or most preferred style, but when that style seems inappropriate in a given situation or does not work, the individual may go to the next preference in the hierarchy, and so on. The self-assessment you just completed identified the hierarchy you used in the specific conflicts you remembered Refer back to that hierarchy as we explore what these various styles mean. Think about the accuracy of your profile and whether it is an effective one for you.

Conflict styles frequently are described as five basic orientations based on the balance between satisfying individual needs and goals and satisfying the needs and goals of others in the conflict.

Avoidance. Individuals preferring the avoidance style are unlikely to pursue their own goals and needs or to support relationships during conflict. Conflict makes them very uncomfortable and often fearful. Although avoiders may have a genuine concern for goals and relationships, they do not see conflict as a positive solution. Avoiders may cope well during times of harmony but refrain-often both psychologically and physically-from participating in conflict situations.

Where was the avoidance style in your personal hierarchy? Can you identify friends or family who have this preferences? How would you describe the impact of avoiders on decision making and on long-term relationships? The question of impact is especially important for organizations. Although most people agree that individuals within organizations have important preferences, organizations employ people to use their skills and abilities-the best of their thinking. When an individual avoids participating in decisions subject to conflict, the organization may lose important information that the individual is essentially responsible for contributing.

Competition. the individual who prefers competition approaches conflict by emphasizing personal goals and needs without considering the opinions or needs of others in the conflict. Competitive individuals often conceptualize conflict as win-lose and prefer to view themselves as winners. This orientation can block good problem solving, particularly if the competitive person needs input on a decision. On a more positive note, when a group is hopelessly deadlocked, competitors often believe it is their responsibility to make a decision and to take responsibility for that decision. Given ability appropriate to the problem, this approach can be organizationally effective.

How often do you use the competitive approach? How effective has it been? Can you visualize a competitor and an avoider in a conflicting situation? What would you predict will occur? Sensitivity to the impact of the competitive approach is especially important because this style can be both abusive or exactly what the organization needs. The strong competitor can be guilty of discounting other good ideas and personally attacking others in order to remain a winner. When an avoider and a competitor disagree, the competitor usually wins, with little or no resistance: but this win is good for the organization only if the competitor was right and had all the appropriate information. Can you think of a time when you really had the best information, even if others disagreed? What type of behavior was needed for an effective decision? How important was it to pursue your point of view? The competitor runs the risk of competing for the sake of competing. However, the competitor can make a decision when others are hopelessly dead-looked. The potential positives and negatives from the competitive style illustrate the need for sensitivity competency in communication. Competent communicators are sensitive to their preferences and the appropriateness of applying them to specific situations. In this case, competency involves knowing when competitiveness is needed and when it is counterproductive.

Compromise. Compromisers prefer to balance people concerns with task issues and often approach conflict with a give-and-take attitude that contributes to negotiation. Most of us can identify numerous times when conflict was managed through compromise. Compromise works because all parties can minimize losses while establishing some gains. indeed, organizations frequently encourage compromise, and it has become a preferred orientation in many decision-making groups.

However, a word of caution is appropriate. Have you ever been involved in a compromise that didn't really work, and the problem surfaced again? Did the compromise represent good problem solving or was it just a convenient and comfortable way out of conflict? As with the competitive approach, a preference for compromise should be matched to the needs of the situation. Individuals who are willing to compromise can help organizations make a decision from among various conflicting viewpoints. If that decision, however, does not represent through problem solving and allows the issue to resurface, the compromise orientation should have been avoided. Look again at your profile. How important is compromise to you? How effective has it been?

Accommodation. People who want to be liked, have high affiliative needs, or genuinely are concerned for the needs of others often prefer an accommodative approach to conflict. Accommodation is characterized by the sacrifice of personal goals in order to maintain relationships. This style can provide important support to groups engaged in making difficult decisions, but it also encourages the accommodative individual to abandon issue, goal, or task input when others appear to disagree.

Naturally, most of us want to be like. But again, the issue organizational effectiveness. Is the accommodative individual withholding an opinion to maintain a relationship with his or her boss or co-workers? How important is that opinion to what happens in the work group? Does the accommodative style keep the individual from being a good contributor or is his or her real contribution the support of others? These are difficult questions requiring both sensitivity and good analysis skills. Think again about the conflicts you identified in your profile. Was accommodation a preference for you or others? How did the accommodative approach work? Should it be used again?

Collaboration. The collaborative style is clearly seen as the ideal because this approach influences individuals to work for goals, to examine issues thoughtfully, and to be task oriented while supporting, others to do the same. On the other hand, collaboration is the most difficult of all the styles to actually use for strategic objectives and tactical behaviors. Individuals who prefer collaboration can only behave collaboratively when others assume a collaborative orientation and have enough task or goal information to solve the problem thoroughly.

Where was the collaborative preference in your hierarchy? Can you see why conflict researchers believe this approach has more merit than avoidance, compromise, competition, or accommodation? Now think back to the specific conflicts you used in your self-analysis. Were these problems handled collaboratively? If these problems were not handled collaboratively, describe what might have been managed differently. Also, return to John's problem at Middlesex Insurance.

Strategic objectives

As Kenneth Thomas has suggested, individuals' strategic objectives in conflict are determined not only by orientations or preferences for conflict styles but also be assessments of the probable outcomes of behavior within particular contexts. Specifically, strategic objectives are determined by matching general preferences for particular conflict styles with assessments of the risks involved in a particular situation. In addition, as Charles Conrad has pointed out, strategic choices are made not only with individual preferences in mind but also with consideration of the communication strategies in mind but also with consideration of the communication strategies used by others involved in the conflict. Organizational role, power positions, previous experiences, and the importance of specific issues all contribute to the strategic objectives adopted by conflict participants.

A strategic choice is, according to Gerald Phillips and Nancy Metzger a "planned method of conducting operations" in order to structure the conflict in one of four strategic directions: escalation, reduction, maintenance, or avoidance. As Joyce Frost and William William Wilmot have suggested, "strategies are the large, general game plans in conflicts, and tactics are the moves made to advance the conflict in the strategic direction that the participants informally and implicitly work out among themselves."

In The Middlesex Insurance Case, as John reflects on his problem with John, he is beginning to establish strategic objectives. His personal preferences and decisions will affect whether the conflict escalates, reduces, stays at the present level, or is avoided. For example, if John chooses to escalate the conflict he can announce that his training schedule will be initiated as announced and that those not in agreement can look for work in other departments. If John has good analysis skills he can predict that this action will probably anger Joan and possibly others. He cannot know with certainty what Joan's reaction will be, but he can assume that conflict escalation is the probable outcome. John might attempt to escalate the conflict if the really wanted John and the others to leave; however, his analysis ability probably will tell him he may be viewed with suspicion if competent people leave a department soon after he becomes manager.

On the other hand, John might attempt to reduce the conflict by asking Joan to help him understand her objections to the timetable for training. He would then be in a position to decide whether her objections were based on department operations or were primarily due to his promotion.

John could attempt to maintain the conflict at its present level by acknowledging that he and Joan have differences. He can suggest that he will try his new ideas while being willing to listen to her objections if there are problems. John will have difficulty in choosing the strategic objective of avoidance because he and Joan have already voiced opposing views. He can, of course, back off of his training schedule and not make further reference to their disagreement.

Communication tactics in conflict

Conflict tactics can be described as communication behaviors that attempt to move the conflict toward escalation, reduction, maintenance at the present level, or avoidance. The tactics adopted are influenced by individual conflict preferences and strategies and by overall organizational values about how conflict is supposed to work. For example powerful individuals frequently use competitive and confrontational tactics, whereas individuals apprehensive about communicating use more avoidance tactics. Some organizations encourage open debate and disagreement, whereas others insist on disagreement only if there are no personal attacks or displays of anger. Still others discourage overt conflict of any type. In any case, the exchanges of communication tactics among conflict participants illustrate the interactive nature of conflict, with outcomes related to complex tactical interactions as well as orientations and strategic objectives.

Although it is impossible to list or define all of the possible tactics available to conflict participants, it is important for out personal sensitivity and also for our verbal skills to identify frequently used conflict tactics. Tactics are grouped into the following categories: tactics for conflict escalation, tactics for conflict avoidance, tactics for conflict maintenance, and tactics for conflict reduction.

Organizational conflicts are characterized by the frequent use of all of these tactics and many more. Furthermore, organizational life brings all of us in contact with individuals who have vastly different conflict styles, strategic objective, and tactical approaches. These differences can either contribute to productive conflict or be a primary reason conflict is destructive, resulting i bad decisions and ultimately additional conflict.

The figure identified frequently used conflict communication tactics through short excerpts from transcripts of organizational conflict. To further develop your sensitivity and skills for tactic identification, the figure provides a more detailed transcript of an organizational conflict. As you read the transcript, try to identify tactics used for escalation, avoidance, maintenance, or reduction. Finally, as you read the transcript think about tactics you use and tactics you have observed.

Index